ACADEMICS
ON STRIKE

James P. Begin
Theodore Settle
Paula Alexander

Institute of Management and Labor Relations
University Extension Division
Rutgers • The State University of New Jersey
In cooperation with
Academic Collective Bargaining Information Service
Washington, D.C.

This is Monograph Number 2

This book was edited and produced for the Institute of Management and Labor Relations, Rutgers University, by J. Carl Cook and Hope M. Fead of the University Extension Division Publications Office. The cover design is by Rose Marie Bratek.

 2

MacCrellish & Quigley Company

CONTENTS

PREFACE AND ACKNOWLEDGMENTS

Over the past eight years, faculty in some 350 institutions of higher education have moved to restructure power relationships by adopting the techniques of collective bargaining. During this time there have been only five occasions when faculty in four-year institutions which were organized for collective bargaining purposes have employed the ultimate bargaining weapon—the strike.

This book deals in depth with two of these occasions. A strike at Rider College (New Jersey) occurred in October 1974, the first collective bargaining strike in a private institution. Another strike took place at the eight New Jersey state colleges in November, 1974. The latter strike was the first affecting a public system of higher education.

To what extent can it be expected that faculty as professionals will adopt the strike weapon as a common means of solving perceived or real problems? How effective will the strike weapon be as a means of resolving faculty bargaining disputes? What are the boundaries of faculty bargaining power? These are the central questions to which the two case studies reported here attempt to provide initial insights.

The data used to analyze the two strikes are drawn from a larger, five-year study of the origins and impact of faculty collective bargaining in New Jersey's private and public system of higher education. The authors express deep appreciation to the following individuals and organizations who have financially supported the study. The project was initially funded by the U.S. Office of Education. For the past three years the research has been funded by the Carnegie Corporation of New York. Alden Dunham and James

Dyer of the Carnegie Corporation have been extremely helpful. The Department of Research of the Institute of Management and Labor Relations, Rutgers University, has also provided substantial support for the project. Thanks especially go to Robert Klein, the director, for agreeing to help support the publication of this book.

The authors are indebted to large numbers of people who have aided the data collection, analysis, and writing. The parties under study have been extremely patient under a constant barrage of interviews and requests for documents. Indeed, the support of the parties at all institutions and all levels of government has been phenomenal. We only wish we had room here to express our appreciation individually.

Thanks are due to Judy von Loewe, Maryjanet Rodriguez, Alida Jagt, Betty Lou Heffernan, and Leona Gyomulcs who ably typed and proofread numerous drafts.

Editorial assistance and publishing arrangements were handled by Jake Cook and Hope Fead, the editors of the Rutgers University Extension Division. The authors also express thanks to Jack Chernick, Harry Stark, and William Weinberg, our colleagues in the Department of Research, Institute of Management and Labor Relations, for their valuable comments on an earlier draft. Barbara Tener, research assistant, was extremely helpful in ordering the state college data.

Finally, George Angell and Edward Kelly, director and assistant director, respectively, of the Academic Collective Bargaining Information Service, Washington, D.C., deserve particular mention for originally suggesting the concept as well as the timing of this book.

The organization of the book is as follows: Chapter I establishes the historical context and sets out the study framework. Chapters II and III will proceed with a detailed description of each strike. It should be noted that, due to the different dynamics of the strikes and the different bargaining histories, variations occur in the formats used in these two chapters. Chapter IV will compare the two strikes, summarize the findings, and draw conclusions about the nature of faculty strikes.

Chapter I

INTRODUCTION

Over the years the strike·has been the ultimate, and most important, source of union power in resolving disputes in the private sector of the United States economy, whether the disputes be over the right to organize or within the bargaining context. Despite legal barriers in most public jurisdictions, public employees have increasingly used the strike weapon as well.[1]

Faculty in some 350 institutions of higher education have responded to changes in enabling legislation and to other conditions external and internal to their particular institutions by adopting collective bargaining as a means of relating to the decision-making structures and processes of these institutions.[2] With the adoption of collective bargaining one would expect also that the strike weapon would be used in resolving disputes. Indeed, early articles on the growth of faculty unionism often created the spectre of faculty "hitting the bricks" to press their bargaining demands.[3]

But the evidence to date indicates that while faculty have adopted collective bargaining, the strike has been used very infrequently. As noted by Carr and Van Eyck, "the strike has never been much used by college teachers as a means of bringing pressure on governing boards, administrators, legislatures, alumni, or society."[4] Before the onset of the faculty bargaining movement, there were work stoppages at St. John's University in New York, Catholic University in Washington, D.C., and at San Francisco State College in California. The St. John's and Catholic University strikes occurred in response to dismissals of faculty by the respective governing boards of the institutions. Faculty demands during the work stoppage were concerned in a major way with greater involvement of faculty in decision making, a professional dimension of employment which is

1

important to faculty.[5] So while the work stoppages did not derive from the collective bargaining context, the issues at St. John's and Catholic University were directly related to issues that could come up in the collective bargaining context under "conditions of employment."

Still, in the first decade of the faculty bargaining movement, there have been only five strikes recorded in four-year institutions. In addition there have been only twenty-five to thirty strikes in two-year institutions.[6] Given the fact that there have been approximately 500 two-year and 150 four-year agreements negotiated over a ten-year period, the level of strike activity can be considered low.[7]

The first strike in a four-year institution which was the product of a bargaining relationship took place four years after the first four-year institution was organized for collective bargaining purposes.[8] The strike, which lasted for two weeks, occurred in September 1971 at Oakland University, a public institution of higher education in Michigan. While the strike at Oakland was an illegal strike since public employee strikes in Michigan are prohibited, the university administration did not elect to seek an injunction. According to Carr and Van Eyck the Oakland strike was primarily over compensation matters.[9] But Professor Pitts of the Oakland faculty suggests that there were deeper organizational problems having to do with the failure of the university to fulfill its proclaimed mission. He stated, "Oakland University was perhaps more affected than many other places because it had conceived of itself as 'the Oberlin of Michigan.' Now it was being called to do much work for which community colleges seemed better equipped. The 'Oakland mystique' was dead, and the road toward becoming another second-rate university was slow and glamourless."[10]

The strike-free period that followed was broken when four strikes occurred in the 1974-75 academic year. The faculty at Rider College, a private school in New Jersey, struck for eight days (six working days) in October, 1974. Interestingly, the American Association of University Professors (AAUP), which on the national level opposes strikes except in extenuating circumstances, was the bargaining agent in both the Rider College strike and the Oakland University strike.

A strike also occurred in the fall of 1974 at the eight New Jersey state colleges. The strike led by the American Federation of Teachers (AFT) lasted ten days in November. The next strike, which lasted

2

for a half day, was at the C.W. Post Center of Long Island University in early 1975. The bargaining agent at this private institution is a merged National Education Association (NEA)-AFT representative. The last strike, lasting for a week in early 1975, also occurred at a private institution, Robert Morris College in Pennsylvania. AFT is the bargaining agent.[11]

Given the integral relationship of collective bargaining and strikes in the private sector of the U.S. economy, and the adoption of collective bargaining by faculty in some institutions of higher education, how do we explain the low incidence of strikes in higher education?

It is the purpose of this book to assess this question by describing and analyzing the causes, effectiveness, and impact of the strikes at Rider College and the New Jersey state colleges which took place in the fall of 1974. The Rider College strike was the first collective bargaining strike to occur in a private institution, and the state college strike was the first to occur in a multi-institutional public system.

FRAMEWORK

The causes, effectiveness, and impact of the two strikes will be analyzed by tracing the historical development of faculty-administration relationships at these institutions, with a particular focus on the factors producing the bargaining relationship and the nature of the bargaining history. The framework used to identify relevant research variables for this study is illustrated in Figure 1.[12]

Generally, it is postulated that faculty's willingness to enter into a bargaining relationship which may lead to their subsequent involvement in strike activity is a product of their job satisfaction. Some of the working conditions thought to be particularly relevant to faculty job satisfaction are listed in Figure 1. It can be expected that faculty bargaining and faculty strikes will be more likely to occur where there is greater generalized faculty discontent in respect to salary, benefits, working conditions, and degree of participation in decision making.

Faculty job satisfaction, in turn, is related to the faculty's understanding of themselves as a profession and therefore as professionals, the organizational context provided by a particular institution and/or system of higher education, and the external environmental forces which affect the operation of an institution or system of higher education.

3

Figure 1
Study Framework*

External Environment→	Organizational Context→	Faculty Job Satisfaction→	Faculty Attitudes and Behavior in Respect to Collective Bargaining→	Bargaining Process→	Impact of Collective Bargaining
State of Economy	Type of Institution	Economic Benefits	Acceptance/Rejection of Collective Bargaining	Bargaining Structure	Rationalization of Policy
Legislation	Type of Control	Academic Freedom	Union Membership	Bargaining Agent	Redistribution of Authority
Demand for Education	Size	Tenure	Willingness To Strike	Scope of Bargaining	Psychological Climate
Bargaining Experiences of Other Institutions	Decision-Making Structure	Decision-Making Authority	Participation in Union Activities	Bargaining Relationship	Resource Allocation
Union Competition	Economic Condition of Institution	Methods of Instruction	Perceived Function of Bargaining in Higher Education	Student Influence	
	Stability	Curriculum Decisions			
		Promotion Procedures			
		Workload			
		Relations with Administration			
		Public Support of Higher Education			
		Relations with Colleagues			

*Note: For ease of presentation, all expected interactions of the variables are not indicated. For full description of framework, see James P. Begin, *Faculty Bargaining, A Conceptual Discussion* (Institute of Management and Labor Relations, Rutgers University, February, 1973).

4

It is hoped that the description and analysis of the two strikes will contribute to an improved understanding of the factors affecting contemporary relationships between faculty as professionals and the increasingly bureaucratic organizations in which they work. Institutions of higher education are often described as having provided through faculty self-governance mechanisms a reasonable balance between professional needs and organizational needs. The unionization of faculty represents, perhaps, a further adaptation of a profession to the bureaucratic organization in which they work.

Another factor likely to be a major *cause* of strike action is the perceived failure of the bargaining process to resolve faculty concerns which initially led to the institution of a bargaining relationship. For this reason, particular attention will be given in this analysis to the forces creating the particular collective bargaining relationship as well as the subsequent negotiation history.

The *effects* of faculty bargaining are conceptualized as the outputs of the bargaining process. As illustrated in Figure 1, it is expected that the faculty bargaining process and the rule changes deriving from the process will lead to the rationalization of management practices; the redistribution of authority among faculty, administrators, and students; changes in the psychological climate; and changes in the resource allocation process. Faculty strike activity will tend to reinforce these consequences of faculty unionism.

The *effectiveness* of faculty strikes will be directly related to faculty bargaining power, that is, the ability of the faculty to inflict economic and noneconomic costs on the other party to negotiations. Bargaining power is a function of all the internal and external factors affecting the bargaining exchange process noted in Figure 1. The following discussion will assess the potential effectiveness of faculty strikes by considering the strike costs borne by the faculty union and its members and by management. The contextual factors which condition the pattern of strike costs will also be discussed.

Employee and Employee Organization Strike Costs

As Walton and McKersie [13] point out, the strike costs borne by employees and their organizations include wage losses, effect on the security of the employee organization through loss of membership and financial resources, loss of goodwill with the management officials, and damage to the public image of the employee organization.

The greatest cost of the work stoppage to any individual is the loss of wages. Since many faculty receive higher wages compared to the typical unionized employee, it could be argued that they would be able to withstand strikes for a longer period of time, assuming that their living expenses were not proportionately higher. However, basic to such a position is an assumption that faculty are disposed to engage in job actions. A nationwide survey conducted by the Carnegie Commission in 1969 indicates that on a perceptual level, strikes are not anathema to faculty. Forty-six percent of the sample responded "definitely yes" or "probably yes" that "there are circumstances in which a strike would be a legitimate means of collective action for faculty members." [14] Unfortunately, the Carnegie data refer only to attitudinal differences within faculty, and do not compare faculty responses to other occupations. So it is difficult to conclude from such data that faculty are either more or less likely to strike than workers in other occupations. But the relatively low level of strike activity to date supports a hypothesis that, on balance, faculty unions will have relatively greater difficulty than many other unions in mounting or sustaining successful strikes unless the issues are perceived by the faculty as directly related to the *loss of control and/or lack of control* over those resources necessary for the acquisition or maintenance of professional status. Figure 1 lists some of the resources likely to be of importance to faculty, for example, salary, academic freedom, tenure and governance procedures.

To the extent that the professional values of the faculty prevent them from initiating and supporting job actions, the bargaining leverage which the faculty negotiators have at hand is reduced. Moreover, faculty negotiators who engage in job actions without the substantial support of the membership might endanger the stability and security of the employee organization. Faculty strike activity might also endanger a union's good will with management, leading to the development of an adversary, polarized relationship. Again, the faculty may be averse to this potential outcome. However, it is also true that strikes often unite diverse elements of a bargaining unit as well as clear the air between union and management (Impact on psychological climate—Figure 1). The faculty organization's public image may also be endangered because, under most circumstances, it is more likely that public sentiment would be against the efforts of comparatively highly-paid professionals to increase their economic well-being, particularly if the strike is illegal.

Management Strike Costs

The costs to management of strike activity consist of loss of profits, loss of status with other management officials, loss of goodwill with labor, and loss of public image.[15]

Since most public and private universities are nonprofit, the question arises as to what the substitute for the profit measure is in the public sector. In the absence of the profit motive, the primary motive for the public employer is to do a responsible job for the taxpayers. However, in some quarters it is argued that the political leaders will overlook the long-run implications of wage settlements to offset short-run political costs of strikes.[16] In other words, political leaders will capitulate in the short run to prevent political costs.

An economic cost to institutions of higher education would be the potential loss of students and tuition revenue from lengthy strikes. The extent of the impact would depend on how much of the expenses are paid by tuition (significantly more at private institutions) and on how long it took to rebuild enrollments. Reportedly, it took Oakland University several semesters to recover lost enrollments, and the institution's budget was correspondingly reduced in the interim. Aside from the loss of tuition dollars, the impact of a strike is difficult to assess due to the well-known problems of trying to measure the returns to education and the factors which affect those returns. But it is safe to say that in comparison with a police strike, the impact of a faculty strike on society is minimal in the short run.

In strike situations the academic administration stands a chance of losing goodwill with the faculty organization—creating an adverse relationship. It is unlikely that the local campus administrators would see this as a desirable goal, given their training in the concept of collegiality. Strike activities by the faculty on university campuses will also probably reinforce the less-than-favorable public image of institutions of higher education which some feel has been developing in recent years. Thus, the potential damage to the public image of the university is great. In sum, the potential economic and noneconomic strike costs borne by an academic administration may be a factor in favor of the faculty organizations, depending on the impact of the contextual factors discussed below.

Contextual Factors and Strike Costs

There are a number of internal and external factors which may affect the operation of the bargaining process and thus the pattern

7

of strike costs in any given set of negotiations: the state of the economy, the economic condition of the institution, the structure of faculty work, the characteristics of the faculty, the type of educational institution, the collective bargaining structure, bargaining legislation, the role of the students, and the nature of the bargaining agent.

Depressed economic conditions in private industry often lead to the development of a cooperative relationship as the parties jointly seek survival of the organization. This pattern will probably repeat itself in private institutions of higher education. But in public institutions it may be more difficult for the faculty to accept economy measures imposed by the state legislature because the ability of faculty to achieve increased benefits is dependent not only upon increasing tuition levels, but also upon the willingness of the legislature and the taxpayer to support rising higher education budgets. In the face of legislators' growing disenchantment with universities and increasing competition for the tax dollar from other social needs, continuing taxpayer support of education may not be favorable to faculty bargaining power.

The *structure of faculty working conditions* appears both to enhance and to diminish faculty bargaining power. The school year covers a finite period and a long strike endangers the ability of an institution to carry out its mission and is particularly disastrous to students. Moreover, during a strike, many faculty are only stopping part of their work: their teaching duties. Their scholarly endeavors, to which many of them assign a higher priority, often are continued. It would be difficult for an administration to continue to operate classes during strikes by employing substitute instructors because the level of expertise in most classes is too high to be easily replaced. On the other hand, the nature of faculty working conditions may work against the effectiveness of faculty bargaining power. For example, tenure gives faculty members a long-run commitment to a particular institution and there is no real threat that they, in large numbers, will find permanent alternate jobs during the strike and not return to work after the strike is over. Indeed, the school-year cycle makes it difficult for professors to find immediate alternate college employment in the same geographical area. The tightening of the labor market in higher education in recent years reduces the mobility of the faculty even more. For students, however, the range of choice of alternate institutions has broadened and the prospect of the students leaving during a prolonged strike is real.

8

There are likely to be major differences among *individuals* and among *different types of educational institutions* in respect to faculty support for strikes. The Carnegie Commission survey in 1969 provides clues about the different perceptions of faculty toward strikes. Faculty from institutions in which the salary levels and the effectiveness of the faculty senate and the administration were evaluated as "excellent" or "good" were less likely to agree that "there are circumstances in which a faculty strike would be legitimate" than those who evaluated these factors as "fair" or "poor."[17] Interestingly, there was little difference in the way faculty from two-year, liberal arts, comprehensive colleges and universities and doctoral-granting institutions answered the same question. From a behavioral perspective, however, the lower incidence of organization among quality institutions indicates that there is less perceived need for faculty to utilize bargaining and the strike weapon in such institutions.

In respect to individual characteristics, the older and the tenured faculty in the Carnegie Commission survey were, not surprisingly, less likely to support bargaining strikes. There was also a high correlation between a faculty member's "self-described political leaning" and support for faculty strikes: faculty with liberal and left leanings were much more supportive of strikes.[18]

An obvious impact of *legislation* on bargaining power is whether the right to strike is limited. With the exception of a few states, public employees do not enjoy the right to strike. In those states where there are public employee statutes which provide public employees the right to bargain without a corresponding right to strike there are usually statutory impasse procedures (mediation and/or fact-finding) for resolving bargaining disputes. Whether these substitute procedures provide public employees with adequate bargaining leverage is a much discussed but undecided issue. While some public employee groups have used the strike weapon, the illegality of strikes no doubt dampens the ability of unions to build faculty support for illegal strikes. The absence of adequate enforcement procedures for unfair labor practices requiring the parties to bargain in good faith is also believed to weaken a union's ability to broaden the scope of negotiations.

One important distinction between the strikes reported in this book is that Rider College is covered by federal legislation which permits strikes, while in New Jersey the state courts have determined that public employees do not have the right to engage in job actions. In addition, there were no administrative procedures for enforcing restrictions against unfair labor practices in the New Jersey public sector bargaining law until recent amendments went into effect on January 20, 1975.

The *collective bargaining structure* can also influence the level of faculty bargaining power. A large statewide bargaining unit, for example, would tend to increase the power of the faculty organizations since all educational institutions in the state could be shut down. Even in states where the strike is illegal, a strike in a large bargaining unit makes it difficult for the public employer to mete out penalties. Another impact of structure is the effect it would have on the ability of students to seek out alternate educational opportunities within the same state. At Oakland the students could easily attend other similar institutions in Michigan since each institution comprised a separate bargaining unit. But at the State University of New York, all public four-year institutions in upstate New York are included in the same bargaining unit, minimizing transfer opportunities and thus strike costs to the institutions. On the other hand, it would be difficult for a bargaining agent to mount a strike in a statewide unit due to the difficulty of achieving solid support because of the diversity of the unit and communications problems, that is, intra-organizational bargaining for the union becomes more difficult.

A bargaining unit encompassing an entire system of higher education could have dysfunctional effects on management as well. The inability of the management team to achieve internal consensus because of a complex, multi-level decision-making structure may enhance the opportunities of bargaining agents to engage in bargaining with various levels of management, that is, to engage in alternate bargaining activities.[19] In a strike situation encompassing a large unit, the political officials (e.g., governor and/or legislature) may be more sensitive to end-running activities, particularly if the administration was elected with labor support and/or does not agree with the bargaining style of lower levels of management.

The *type of bargaining agent* may also influence the impact of a strike. For example, another interesting difference between Rider College and the New Jersey state colleges is that the national organizations of the two local bargaining agents have differing views toward the use of strikes. The AFT has no qualms about using the strike, while the AAUP discourages the use of strikes except where ". . . situations may arise affecting a college or university which so flagrantly violate academic freedom (of students as well as of faculty) or the principles of academic government, or which are so resistant to rational methods of discusison, persuasion, and conciliation, that faculty members may feel impelled to express their condemnation by withholding their services. . ."[20]

A unique aspect of collective bargaining in institutions such as colleges, schools, welfare agencies, and prisons is that the relationship between the producer and the product is a human relationship. In respect to strikes, *the role of students* in affecting the balance of power is difficult to predict. At Oakland student rowdyism reportedly became a concern to both sides. Student support is likely to flow with the issues. For example, where there is a more direct relationship between costs of bargaining gains and tuition levels, e.g., in private institutions, the students would be more likely to support administrative positions and pressure faculty to end the strike. Similarly in prolonged strikes students may develop a generalized opposition to the strike out of a concern for losing course credits, and decide to put pressure on one or both parties to settle. At this point in the development of faculty bargaining, the most that can be said about the role of students in strikes is that if students choose to exercise their influence by adding another voice to negotiations (alternate bargaining), they are likely to be a major factor in forcing faculty-administration accommodations.

DISCUSSION OF STUDY AND METHODS

The data used to analyze the strikes at Rider College and the New Jersey state colleges are derived from a longitudinal case study of the New Jersey public and private system of higher education. Since 1969 the Department of Research of the Institute of Management and Labor Relations, Rutgers University, has been documenting the development of the faculty bargaining movement across the United States, with particular attention to New Jersey institutions of higher education. The New Jersey research effort was supported initially by the U.S. Office of Education and for the past three years by the Carnegie Corporation of New York.[21]

Currently in New Jersey there are eighteen college faculty bargaining units covering twenty-five public institutions and five units covering five private institutions. All public colleges and universities in New Jersey are organized with the exception of one community college. The eight state colleges are included in one comprehensive

11

bargaining unit, while single units are located at: Rutgers University (AAUP), the College of Medicine and Dentistry of New Jersey (AAUP), the New Jersey Institute of Technology (Independent), and fourteen community colleges (four AFT, ten NEA). Monmouth College (NEA), Bloomfield College (AAUP), Union College (AAUP), Rider College (AAUP), and Fairleigh Dickinson University (AAUP) comprise the five independent institutions of a total of twenty-six in New Jersey now bargaining. Since 1966 higher education in New Jersey has been coordinated by the Board of Higher Education and its administrative arm, the Department of Higher Education.

The major questions which the research project of which this study is a part attempt to answer are: Why have faculty at these institutions chosen to organize; what have been the consequences to the organization of the faculty bargaining movement?

The data base to answer these questions has been developed from over 600 structured and unstructured interviews, direct observation of over 500 meetings related to the bargaining and governance processes, content analysis of hundreds of documents related to the history and evolution of the bargaining and governance processes, and a statewide questionnaire survey of faculty perceptions in the public institutions.

In addition to the historical data collected over a period of years, interviews were conducted with the parties at Rider and the New Jersey state colleges before, during, and subsequent to the strike. Faculty on the picket lines were interviewed at all campuses. Documents specifically related to the strike were also analyzed.

The following chapter will deal with the institution where the faculty struck first—Rider College.

NOTES

[1] The number of strikes in the public sector increased thirteen times between 1965 and 1971. U.S. Department of Labor, *Analysis of Work Stoppages, 1971,* Bulletin 1777 (Washington, D.C.: Government Printing Office, 1973) , p. 7.

[2] Edward P. Kelley, Jr., *Special Report #12* (Washington, D.C.: Academic Collective Bargaining Information Service, February, 1975) .

[3] Myron Lieberman, "Professors, Unite!," *Harper's Magazine,* October, 1971, pp. 61-70.

[4] Robert K. Carr and Daniel K. Van Eyck, *Collective Bargaining Comes to the Campus* (Washington, D.C.: American Council on Education, 1973) , p. 169.

[5] Ibid., pp. 180-82.

[6] Thomas A. Emmett, special assistant to the president, Regis College, in a personal letter to authors, May 13, 1975, identified twenty-two strikes for which he had information. He felt that there probably were more.

7 This is an approximate, though probably conservative, estimate based on the fact that there were 142 two-year and 56 four-year contracts in effect in February, 1975. Kelley, *Special Report #12.*

8 The U.S. Merchant Marine Academy (AFT) appears to have been the first four-year institution organized (1967) .

9 Carr and Van Eyck, *Collective Bargaining Comes to Campus,* pp. 183-86.

10 Jesse R. Pitts, "Strike at Oakland University," *Change,* February, 1972, p. 17.

11 *Chronicle of Higher Education,* April 21, 1975, p. 2.

12 For more detailed discussion of framework, see James P. Begin, *Faculty Bargaining: A Conceptual Discussion* (Institute of Management and Labor Relations, Rutgers University, February, 1973) .

13 Richard E. Walton and Robert B. McKersie, *A Behavioral Theory of Labor Negotiations* (New York: McGraw-Hill, 1965) , p. 31.

14 Carnegie Commission, *Governance of Higher Education* (New York: McGraw-Hill Book Co., 1973) , p. 42.

15 Walton and McKersie, *A Behavioral Theory of Labor Negotiations,* p. 31.

16 For example, see Harry H. Wellington and Ralph K. Winter, *The Unions and the Cities* (Washington, D.C.: Brookings Institution, 1971) .

17 Carnegie Commission, *Governance of Higher Education,* p. 42.

18 Ibid.

19 James P. Begin, *Faculty Bargaining: A Conceptual Discussion* (Institute of Management and Labor Relations, Rutgers University, February, 1973) , under the heading, "Alternate Bargaining," pp. 51-64. See especially the subsection headed "Management Factionalism." See also in relation to this, the developing literature on multilateral bargaining: Kenneth McLennan and Michael H. Moskow, "Multilateral Bargaining in the Public Sector," *Proceedings of the Twenty-First Annual Winter Meetings* (Madison, Wis.; Industrial Relations Research Association, 1968) ; Michael H. Moskow, J. Joseph Loewenberg, and Edward J. Kozaria, *Collective Bargaining in Public Employment* (New York: Random House, 1970) ; Thomas A. Kochan, "A Theory of Multilateral Collective Bargaining in City Governments," *Industrial and Labor Relations Review,* Vol. 27, No. 4 (July, 1974) , pp. 525-542.

20 American Association of University Professors, "Statement on Faculty Participation in Strikes," *AAUP Policy Documents and Reports* (Washington, D.C.: American Association of University Professors, 1973) , p. 56.

21 While the study was made possible by funds from the U.S. Office of Education and the Carnegie Corporation, the statements made and views expressed are solely the responsibility of the authors.

Chapter II

THE RIDER COLLEGE STRIKE

On October 16, 1974, the faculty of Rider College, a private institution in Trenton, New Jersey, commenced what was to be an eight-day strike (six working days), affecting 5,500 students and 200 faculty. The strike, led by the Rider Chapter of the American Association of University Professors, was the first to occur in a private institution in the context of a collective bargaining relationship since the National Labor Relations Board assumed jurisdiction over private institutions of higher education in 1970.[1] It was the second faculty strike in four-year institutions of higher education in which the faculty were organized for collective bargaining purposes.

The strike at Rider College, which was overwhelmingly supported by the faculty, occurred during negotiations for the first contract and represented the culmination of thirteen and one-half months of bargaining. Faculty support of collective bargaining and of the strike at Rider College is particularly interesting since private institutions generally have been much slower than public institutions to adopt collective bargaining techniques. As of February 1975, only forty, or 3 percent, of the private four-year institutions of higher education were bargaining. Moreover, in 38 percent of the elections in private four-year institutions the faculty have voted against collective bargaining. In contrast, 19 percent of the public four-year institutions are bargaining and only 7 percent of the elections have resulted in the rejection of collective bargaining.[2]

To understand the reasons why Rider College appears to deviate from the norm of other private institutions in respect to collective bargaining activity, it is necessary to trace the events, perceptions, and motivations that initially led the Rider College faculty to organize into a collective bargaining unit. The issues and the lack of satis-

14

factory (to the faculty) solutions to these issues led the faculty to seek out a collective bargaining relationship with the administration. Faculty mistrust of the administration which developed around these issues was not dispelled by the formation of a collective bargaining unit and by subsequent negotiations and was an important ingredient in the mixture of events and attitudes leading to failure to agree and thus the strike.

RIDER COLLEGE: HISTORY AND ORGANIZATION

Rider College had its origins in the business school movement of the 1850s and 1860s.[3] It was founded in 1865 by two business school entrepreneurs as the Trenton Business School, one of forty-five such schools in different cities. In 1897 the school was incorporated as Rider Business College by Andrew Rider, who had joined the institution in 1866, and three of his associates.

In 1898 Franklin B. Moore assumed a faculty position and that same year "acquired Mr. Rider's interest in the school."[4] Thus began the Moore family's involvement in the school which was to last close to seventy years. After merging with another business school in 1901, the name became the Rider-Moore and Stewart School of Business.[5] In 1921 the name was changed to Rider College[6]

During the 1920s Rider's concentration in the business area increased. The New Jersey Board of Education granted Rider College the authority to grant the degrees of Bachelor of Accounts and Bachelor of Commercial Science, and later, the master's degree in accounts and in commercial science.

Franklin F. Moore succeeded his father, Franklin B. Moore, as president in 1934. He soon created the first governing board. A few years later the acts of incorporation were amended to state that "no part of the net earnings of the corporation shall inure to the benefit of any private shareholder or individual."[7] An early indication of Franklin F. Moore's desire to achieve academic recognition for Rider College is represented by his attempt to gain accreditation from the Middle States Association of Secondary Schools and Colleges in the mid-thirties. He found that they had no standards for evaluating specialized schools such as Rider College.

In the 1950s the college administrators found themselves faced with two basic dilemmas. (1) In the face of the tremendous demand being placed on them by growing numbers of applicants, they found

15

it increasingly difficult to find adequate space to increase college enrollment continually. (2) In terms of insuring continued growth and achieving academic recognition, sensitivity to the need to achieve accreditation was greatly heightened.

> One of the outstanding problems confronting the college early in the fifties was that the image of the institution was not favorable. The president of the college, in reflecting on this situation said:

> Although the College had seventeen buildings situated in the City of Trenton, the citizens of the area looked at the main college building at the corner of East State and Carroll Streets and still thought of the college in terms of a business school.[8]

Steps were taken to improve the image of the college. When, in 1952, the accrediting agency of the middle states opened its membership to professional schools other than engineering and teachers' colleges, President Moore, with the support of a significant number of the faculty, requested that Rider College be evaluated. The evaluation and subsequent accreditation took place early in 1955.

Two recommendations of the middle states' evaluation were basic to the formation of the college's future. (1) "It is possible that there exists in the Trenton area a need for another four-year liberal arts college and that Rider might eventually move in that direction," and (2) "In spite of the fact that the existing arrangement (physical plant) has served amazingly well for many years, it might be advisable for Rider College to start from scratch and build a new plant."[9]

The suggestion to rebuild served as a catalyst and by the 1964-65 academic year relocation to a new suburban campus was completed.

During this period of time Rider College received approval (1957) "to confer the degree of Bachelor of Arts in three major fields— English, history and the behavioral sciences." In the same year the Rider College Department of Education offered a program leading to the Bachelor of Arts degree in secondary education. With these new programs Rider departed from its ninety-three year concentration on business education alone.[10]

As an indication of the desire to upgrade the student body, applicants for admission to Rider College in September 1963, were required, for the first time, to submit scores on the Scholastic Aptitude Tests of the College Entrance Examination Board.

Today Rider College is made up of four schools: business administration, education, evening, and liberal arts and sciences, with a total enrollment of approximately 5,500 students. Among the full-time faculty, 72 percent have their appropriate terminal degree.

The shift in the primary emphasis of the college from a business college to a liberal arts college and the concurrent emphasis on upgrading the quality of the faculty (as measured by the number having doctorates or other appropriate terminal degrees) were changes which had major implications for ongoing faculty-administration relationships.

ORIGINS OF BARGAINING

While the movement toward establishment of the faculty collective bargaining unit was initiated and culminated under the current administrative leadership (Dr. Frank N. Elliott became president in August 1969), earlier events and interpretations of those events had a tremendous impact on the developing relationship between the new administration and the faculty.

Prior to August 1969, the office of president of Rider College had been filled consecutively by a father-son team for a period of seventy-one years. Under their leadership the institution experienced significant growth, in part because the persons responsible for public higher education in New Jersey had not responded to the increasing demand for higher education.

During the accreditation process in 1955, President Moore became more aware of the standards used to judge quality faculty through an introduction to AAUP principles concerning promotion and tenure. One outcome of this awareness was a policy that promotion to associate professor required a terminal degree. Achieving tenure, however, did not appear to be similarly constrained; the board of trustees granted tenure to several faculty members in 1963 who had not been promoted to associate professor and who did not hold the doctorate.[11]

In 1967 the business school applied for accreditation from the American Association of Collegiate Schools of Business and found one standard it could not meet: 50 percent of those faculty teaching in the graduate program were required to have the Ph.D. degree. Because of this, greater emphasis was placed upon encouraging currently-employed faculty to obtain the doctorate degree, and on hiring faculty who already held the doctorate.[12]

Also in 1967 President Moore, upon recommendation of the faculty, requested the adoption of the 1940 AAUP statement on promotion and tenure, but with the provision that it not become effective until 1974. The board of trustees approved. The interpretation and application of this policy on promotion and tenure, under President Elliott's leadership, formed one of the basic underlying factors over which conflict and disagreement between the administration and the faculty occurred.

In addition to the issues related to promotion and tenure, there were three other decision areas over which severe disagreement arose. These decision areas were:

(1) *Decisions relative to faculty evaluation.* Along with the emphasis placed on increasing the quality of the faculty by increasing the number who held appropriate terminal degrees, President Elliott notified the faculty that he would also place emphasis on the development of criteria to evaluate the overall activity of the faculty. Annual evaluation of faculty tied to merit pay increases was implemented prior to the full development of objective criteria and evaluation was perceived by the faculty as arbitrary and uneven. The perceived arbitrariness and unevenness of these evaluations, especially when tied to compensation, along with the ongoing disagreements over promotion and tenure issues served as a basis for the developing faculty mistrust of administration motives. The issues related to faculty evaluation, i.e., purpose, content, initiative, and frequency, were among those issues which were not resolved in thirteen and one-half months of negotiations leading ultimately to the faculty strike.

(2) *Appointment of administrators.* Initially the disagreement was not so much over the nature and degree of faculty involvement in these appointments but rather disillusionment with the president's unwillingness to abide by the recommendation of the college search and screening committee he established. Initial disillusionment over the appointment of a vice president for academic affairs led to an increased sensitivity on the part of the faculty to the nature and degree of faculty involvement in administrative appointments, as evidenced by the lengthy discussion in the faculty senate of the proposed changes in the by-laws and statutes of Rider College.

(3) *Resource allocation.* The issue here was the degree of involvement of the faculty in resource allocation decisions. Related to this was the question of budget information. Faculty members of the Budget Priorities Committee strenuously objected to the fact that they were asked to represent the faculty in setting budget priorities

without, at the same time, being given the budget information they felt necessary to fulfill this task responsibly.

The administration's position had been that the process of putting the budget together takes months. Anyone not involved in that process, i.e., faculty, would look at the end product and would make some "erroneous judgments." The administration did not want to spend a great deal of time dealing with these judgments or second guesses.

An underlying theme running through all of these decision areas was the disagreement over the nature and degree of faculty involvement in Rider College's decision-making processes. The faculty attempted to apply quite literally the AAUP "Statement on Government of Colleges and Universities, 1966."[13] The administration perceived the faculty as understanding the collegial decision-making process "to mean that whatever a majority of faculty decided was appropriate was the action that should be taken and that to act otherwise was to be arbitrary, unilateral, and generally non-collegial."[14] Adding to and perhaps aggravating the discussion of these issues was the uncertainty on campus created by a shifting of the college's statement of mission and goals, the general unrest among students also claiming a greater share in decision making, and the growing problems facing institutions of higher education, especially private institutions. The outcome of the prolonged and often heated disagreement over the nature and degree of faculty involvement in the college's decision making and the continuous frustration felt by elected faculty leaders who attempted to make the collegial process work was the turning of the faculty to the only alternative they felt was left to them—participation in decision making through collective bargaining with the administration.

A detailed account of the events in each of these decision areas follows.

Promotion and Tenure

During most of President Moore's term of office, the faculty did not participate either in setting policy or in implementing policy regarding the tenure and promotion processes. However, with the increased "sensitivity" to academic standards brought about through the accreditation process in 1955, President Moore became aware of the "1940 Statement of Principles on Academic Freedom and Tenure."

This sensitivity to the 1940 statement became the basis for further action in 1963, when,

> President Moore and Provost Leonard A. Olson (now deceased) compiled a list of faculty members who had served at Rider College in a full-time capacity since 1954. After they consulted with the deans and department chairmen, other names were added to the list. The designated faculty members then received letters informing them that they had tenure. The list of those on tenure as of September, 1963, contained fifty-one names (including twelve assistant professors, one instructor, and two members of the library staff, none of whom, at that point, held the doctorate).[15]

In doing this President Moore acted to conform to the 1940 statement adopted by the AAUP. However, the 1940 statement was not a part of the bylaws and/or statutes of Rider College. In 1967 the local chapter of the AAUP recommended that the 1940 statement be adopted as the official position of the college.[16] This recommendation went from the Rider AAUP chapter to the board of trustees, who in turn sent it to the faculty senate. The faculty senate endorsed the Rider AAUP chapter proposal at its meeting on May 10, 1967, and in a letter to President Moore requested him to submit the proposal to the board of trustees. At this time President Moore suggested a basic change in the original Rider AAUP chapter proposal. Instead of being implemented immediately, he asked that the implementation of the 1940 statement be delayed until the beginning of the 1974-75 academic year. The Rider AAUP chapter president sent the following memo to President Moore following the October 25, 1967, regular meeting of the Rider AAUP chapter:

> I am happy to report that at our recent meeting of the Rider AAUP Chapter, October 25, 1967, the members voted unanimously to accept the alternate proposal of the administration, which stipulates that our tenure proposal would commence in 1974. We believe that this date is fair to all concerned and are particularly pleased that the administration has acted so promptly in dealing with this important matter.[17]

The alternate proposal was passed by the Rider College Board of Trustees in their November 15, 1967, meeting. The Rider AAUP chapter response, as indicated in their Rider College chapter *AAUP Post*, was as follows:

At its regular November 15, 1967 meeting the Board of Trustees unanimously passed a tenure proposal based on a recommendation initiated by AAUP and passed by the Faculty Senate.

In effect the tenure proposal means that beginning in 1974 a tenure decision will be made by the College for any non-tenured faculty member who at that time has seven years full-time teaching experience. This brings our academic institution in line with the 1940 Statement of Principles on Academic Freedom and Tenure prepared by the Association of American Colleges and the American Association of University Professors.

We applaud this as a good example of working cooperation between the AAUP, Faculty Senate, Administration and Trustees.[18]

What understanding was shared by faculty and administration at that time about the meaning and implications of this policy change is not clear. President Moore intended the seven years (from 1967-1974) as a fair amount of time for those who did not already possess an appropriate terminal degree, to gain one.[19] Whether or not the same meaning can be attached to the statement of the AAUP Rider chapter president, "We believe that this date (1974) is fair to all concerned . . . ," is not as clear. For the faculty were well aware that the granting of tenure in the past was not tied inflexibly to having a doctorate.

Regardless of the degree to which the implications of the alternate resolution were discussed and shared, what became important was the subsequent interpretation made by President Elliott and his administration and the resulting faculty response.

Frank Elliott, as president-elect of Rider College (early 1969), was aware of the proviso making the 1940 statement applicable beginning 1974. He was also aware that only 40 percent of the faculty at Rider College would have an appropriate terminal degree when he took office in August 1969. In his initial convocation address before the faculty he stated:

Hear me carefully because what I am about to say might easily be misunderstood. Each element of the Rider family has said that it would like to see the quality of instruction and the reputation of the college improved. If Rider is to move from being a predominantly teaching to a more quality conscious institution, we must start looking for those traits generally associated with 'quality.' And, it is no secret that many

21

members of the Rider family feel that we must begin evaluating 'quality' in faculty more along lines that are pursued in our most prestigious institutions. Put baldly, this means putting an emphasis on terminal degrees, research and publications. However, even though we emphasize these characteristics in looking for new faculty, the College clearly has a moral obligation to honor commitments made to faculty members who were recruited at a different time and for different purposes. In other words, faculty improvement is clearly an area in which haste will be self-defeating unless it is made slowly and with considered judgment.[20]

In the same convocation address he indicated that he was establishing an ad hoc committee on evaluation comprised of two administrators, five faculty and two students (this committee and its report became known respectively as the 2-5-2 committee and the 2-5-2 report). The purpose of this committee was to study the problem of faculty evaluation and to make recommendations "concerning the criteria and tools to be used to evaluate the levels of teaching skills and research that will warrant promotion and/or tenure."[21]

These two statements along with the progress reports on the percent of the faculty having appropriate terminal degrees in the annual report of the president are a clear indication of a primary goal set by the president and one of the basic indicators he used of progress toward that goal.[22] The goal was building a high quality faculty. The indicator was the percent of faculty having an appropriate (usually Ph.D.) terminal degree. While some of this change could come about by attrition and the hiring of new faculty who already possessed the terminal degree, there was still the question of those faculty who prior to or by 1974 would be beginning their eighth year as full-time faculty members and thus receive automatic tenure under the 1940 statement.

President Elliott chose to interpret the 1967 resolution passed by the board of trustees similarly to President Moore's intention, i.e., that the time from 1967 to 1974 was provided to enable those who had not yet earned the appropriate terminal degree to do so. And this interpretation became the lever used to push those faculty to obtain their degrees or face termination. (A substantial number of these faculty did complete their degrees and were tenured under this policy. However, the faculty perceived the application of this policy as uneven. Thus even the application became an issue.)

The ad hoc committee on evaluation submitted its report to the president in June 1970. In the fall the faculty senate reviewed it and passed several resolutions showing substantial approval of the report. However, the report did not deal clearly with those who already had begun or would begin their eighth year as full-time members of the faculty prior to 1974. In a separate action faculty members of the Rider chapter of the AAUP adopted a resolution "affirming the support of the 1940 *Statement of Principles* and urging acknowledgment of the tenure of all faculty members at the college who had served over seven years."[23] This resolution was sent both to the president and to the faculty senate.

President Elliott responded to the Rider AAUP chapter on November 3, 1970, rejecting its position. He referred it to the resolution passed in 1967 and indicated that full adherence to the 1940 statement would begin in 1974. In support of his position he quoted from the memo President Moore had received from the then (1967) president of the Rider AAUP chapter indicating its support of that resolution.

The faculty senate, knowing the president's response to the Rider AAUP chapter, adopted a similar resolution, urging that all members of the faculty who had finished seven years of acceptable teaching at the college be granted tenure without further delay.

The Daiute Case. At the same time the faculty were discussing the report of the ad hoc committee on evaluation, Professor Robert Daiute was applying for tenure and promotion. Professor Daiute had come to Rider College in 1960 and had been a full-time faculty member since that time. When he came very few of his colleagues in the division of business had doctoral degrees. He alleges he was told that for promotion to associate professor he would need a doctorate, but for tenure the same requirement would not necessarily hold. However, in 1967, the same year the board of trustees passed the resolution regarding the 1940 statement, the division of business was expanded into the School of Business Administration.

When the dean of the School of Business Administration applied for accreditation from the American Association of Collegiate Schools of Business, he was told that at least 50 percent of the faculty teaching in the graduate program would have to hold the doctorate in order for the program to be accredited. Faced with this standard, a new emphasis was placed on faculty having the doctoral degree. Professor Daiute was among those who were encouraged to begin doctoral work. "Professor Daiute refused, asserting that he had been assured earlier that the doctorate would not be an issue in his continuing at the college and that his publications were more than the equivalent of the doctorate."[24]

Following Professor Daiute's application for promotion and tenure in the fall of 1970, the dean of the business school made a negative evaluation of his performance and recommended that he be given a terminal contract for the 1971-72 academic year. This recommendation came at the same time the faculty through the Rider AAUP chapter and the faculty senate were passing resolutions that persons such as Professor Daiute, who had completed at least seven years of teaching at Rider College, be granted tenure immediately.

Professor Daiute's request for promotion and tenure also began to proceed through the promotion and tenure processes which were established on the basis of the report of the ad hoc committee on evaluation. The final decision on Professor Daiute was not made during the 1970-71 academic year. Many committee meetings were held and much time spent on this decision. It was not until December 14, 1971, that the vice president for academic affairs sent him official notice that his contract for academic year 1972-73 would be a terminal one.[25] During this time the issue became not so much whether Professor Daiute was going to be tenured and/or promoted, but whether the collegial process involving peer review would work at Rider College.

The faculty perception of this is seen quite clearly in the discussion held in a faculty senate meeting, February 15, 1972. A resolution regarding Professor Daiute was on the floor. During the discussion it was pointed out that there were three possible interpretations of the resolution as it was worded: (1) an endorsement of Professor Daiute; (2) an endorsement of the 1940 statement; (3) an endorsement of the collegial process in which five of six faculty committees recommended Professor Daiute for tenure. The resolution was changed to reflect the third interpretation: "Be it resolved, that because of the unanimous endorsement of the relevant faculty committees, Professor Robert Daiute be tenured by the Board of Trustees."[26]

During their discussion the faculty senate touched on a basic issue over which there was much disagreement between the faculty and the administration, i.e., the nature of the collegial peer review process, and, even more important, the nature of the total collegial decision-making process. The administration on the issue of peer review with respect to tenure felt that the faculty were not participating in "a true peer review but rather a doctrinaire vote based on the fact that, past understandings to the contrary, seven years meant tenure regardless of the merits of the individual case."[27] The president had stated earlier, "Tenure in particular must be conferred with great care since it represents such a substantial mortgage on an institution's future. When tenure is conferred on a thirty-five year old faculty member, it means that during the succeeding thirty years the College will commit approximately 6,000 students and a minimum of $500,000 to that person."[28]

After the implementation of the ad hoc report of the committee on evaluation (1970), the faculty kept what it called a "scorecard." In this scorecard the faculty compared their recommendation on promotion and tenure with the action of the board of trustees. During the 1970-71 academic year, the first year of the committee on promotion and tenure, the scorecard looked like this:

1970-71 Scorecard on Promotion and Tenure

	Total Applications	Committee on Promotion and Tenure			Board of Trustees		
		Supported	Not Supported	No Vote	Supported	Not Supported	Holding
Tenure	21	16	5	. .	14(1)*	6	. .
Promotion . .	20	15	5	. .	5	15	. .
Prof.	5	4	1	. .	0	5	. .
Associate Prof.	15	11	4	. .	5	10	. .

* One person who was tenured was recommended for tenure by the school committee. The collegewide Promotion and Tenure Committee verbally raised the question as to whether this person's degree was appropriate to the person's present functions but made no recommendation pro or con.

The committee attached a footnote to the scorecard report which read:

> It should be noted that among the candidates denied promotion were nine who had received the unanimous endorsement of all elements in the evaluation process other than the President, i.e., the unanimous vote of the departmental or school committee, the department chairman, the dean, and the committee on Promotion and Tenure.

Among the recommendations made by this committee was this one:

. . . we would recommend that preliminary conferences on all cases be held by the Committee with the President prior to his arriving at a final decision and the submission of his recommendations to the Board of Trustees.[29]

The committee members also indicated that they were quite upset by the difference between the recommendations made by faculty and the action of the board of trustees.

The next year's (1971-72) scorecard read: [30]

1971-72 Scorecard on Promotion and Tenure

| | Total Applications | Committee on Promotion and Tenure | | | Board of Trustees | | |
		Supported	Not Supported	No Vote	Supported	Not Supported	Holding
Tenure	16	14	2	..	9	7	..
Promotion ..	18	6(4)*	8	..	5	13	..
Professor ..	6	1(2)	3	..	1	5	..
Associate Prof. ...	12	5(2)	5	..	4	8	..

*Number in parentheses represents persons supported but not unanimously by the faculty committee.

The faculty senate executive committee commented on this scorecard as follows:

This past year the Promotion and Tenure Committee subjected candidates to rigorous scrutiny, unanimously endorsing only six of eighteen candidates for promotion. The administration rejected every candidate for promotion against whom any single member of the Promotion and Tenure Committee voted as well as a candidate endorsed unanimously by the committee, his dean, his chairman, and his colleagues. The administration also rejected five of the fourteen candidates for tenure that the committee supported.

They add in a parenthetical expression:

(It should be noted that a chief charge against former President Heussler of Trenton State when his faculty censured him last year as phrased in the "No Confidence Petition," was that "approximately one third of the most highly recommended faculty were omitted from the final promotion list).[31]

During the year (1971-72) in the face of Professor Daiute's unsuccessful efforts to gain tenure and again faced with wide dis-

26

crepancies between the committee's recommendations and administrative action, the following resolution was passed indicating the perception of the faculty concerning the operation of the collegial governance structure:

> Whereas the Rider College administration has ignored faculty committee recommendations not consonant with its views and has readily accepted recommendations consonant with its views, in the interest of restoring meaningful faculty governance, be it resolved that the faculty be primarily responsible for appointments, reappointments, decisions not to reappoint, promotions, the granting of tenure, and dismissal. Be it resolved, that the Board of Trustees and the president on matters of faculty status as in other matters where the faculty has primary responsibility, concur with faculty judgment, except in rare instances and for compelling reasons stated in written detail.[32]

This resolution was part of a larger statement which expressed faculty dissatisfaction with the administration's actions in several areas. Prior to the above mentioned action (taken at the faculty association meeting on February, 1972), the senate executive committee had sent out a letter to all faculty citing what they regarded "as a persistent pattern of unilateral administrative decisions." And continuing they stated:

> Your Senate Executive Committee has reached an impasse in its working relation with President Elliott and the administration of Rider College. It is our unanimous judgment that President Elliott has consistantly demonstrated a disregard for points of view that he does not share, and an unwarranted faith in his own evaluative powers when supplied with only a minimum of information; that he has repeatedly usurped prerogatives generally acknowledged to be the faculty's—for example as particularized in the 1966 *Statement on Government of Colleges and Universities* endorsed by the American Association of University Professors, The American Council on Education, and the Association of Governing Boards of Universities and Colleges.[33]

There followed in the letter an indication that the senate executive committee the previous year, already somewhat alarmed, had written a similar letter, but had not sent it out, because they had obtained certain concessions from the president which had enabled the committee to hope that he would subsequently pay more heed to faculty positions. The 1971-72 senate executive committee perceived a year later that this was not the case, and therefore a letter was sent

27

listing what the faculty senate executive committee perceived to be administrative actions incongruous with the administration's espousal of collegial governance.

The faculty senate executive committee's feelings on this are indicated in the following quote:

> An authoritarian college administration, though repugnant to many, is tolerable if two conditions prevail: that its authoritarianism is acknowledged; that it is benevolent. There is significant evidence that neither condition exists at Rider. President Elliott pays lip-service to collegiality—to faculty involvement in college government. His support of the elaborate faculty committee structure worked out by the Stroh Committee indicates so; as does his reply to the AAUP questionnaire (included on the chart published in the March 1971 *AAUP Bulletin*) about faculty participation, in which he declares that matters like appointments, reappointments or nonrenewal, promotions, and tenure are arrived at by joint action of administration and faculty at Rider. His graph has a very democratic profile. The evidence, however, argues that he has consistently overridden duly authorized groups when his opinions differed.[34]

This letter was significant in that it represented the beginning of the objectivation of a faculty position vis-à-vis the administration. This letter formed the basis (for a faculty perspective) not only for interpreting past faculty-administration transactions, but also for future transactions. Even those faculty who had no direct contact with the administration reflecting such instances could not escape (as faculty) being influenced by the continuous presentation of the administration as in fact authoritarian even in the face of the administration's continuous espousal of collegiality.

On December 5, 1972, the Committee on Promotion and Tenure sent a memo to the faculty senate. This memo contained the 1972-73 scorecard.[35]

1972-73 Scorecard on Promotion and Tenure

	Total Applications	Committee on Promotion and Tenure			Board of Trustees		
		Supported	Not Supported	No Vote	Supported	Not Supported	Holding
Tenure	25	22	2	1	13	6	6
Promotion ...	22	15	6	1	12	10	..
Full Prof. .	8	4	4	..	1	7	..
Assoc. Prof.	14	11	2	1	11	3	..

What turned out to be of significance in that year's scorecard were the six persons placed on hold regarding the decision for tenure. This became evident when the six were denied tenure along with another member of the faculty. In March 1973 the whole issue of the faculty's involvement in matters of promotion and tenure came to a head. Not only was there at issue the influence the faculty were to have over promotion and tenure decisions, but also the perceived unwillingness of the administration to deal fairly and honestly with them. The faculty senate minutes of March 13, 1973, read:

From the committee on promotion and tenure to the Faculty Senate: The following statement expressed the collective concerns of the committee on promotion and tenure in regard to administrative action taken on behalf of seven colleagues. (1) recently, seven colleagues were given terminal contracts. Each was eligible for tenure and had received the endorsement of the tenuring hierarchy, i.e., peer groups, department chairmen, etc.; (2) until receipt of the terminal contract our colleagues were placed in a hold category with the additional time ostensibly devoted to an individual, in depth review of accomplishments, academic progress, etc. (3) the administration has repeatedly stated that our colleagues were treated as individuals, and that their tenure applications were judged within the statutes. To this the committee on promotion and tenure must take exception. Until proven otherwise, we must take the position that tenure was denied because the seven did not possess the terminal degree, for this degree appears to be the common denominator in each case. (4) Were the terminal degree a prerequisite for tenure, the foregoing statement would be inappropriate. However, the committee on promotion and tenure must emphasize that the terminal degree is not a prerequisite for tenure, and therefore the committee must object strongly to the application of nonexistent standards. (5) Finally, the administrative actions concerning the seven colleagues leave certain questions that must be answered: (a) If the common denominator in the seven cases was not the absence of a terminal degree, then what characteristics must a colleague possess to be considered an exception under tenure statutes? (b) is the activity of various groups within the tenure process redundant and superfluous?[36]

Subsequent to this time, most of those who were placed in the hold position and were given conditional terminal contracts completed their terminal degree and/or were tenured. However, this did not happen prior to the vote of the faculty to organize for collective bargaining.

National AAUP Intervention. At the same time this was happening, events related to the Daiute case were also coming to a head. During the review process Professor Daiute sought the intervention of the northeast regional office of the AAUP on his behalf. When it became evident that Professor Daiute would not be tenured, the national AAUP organized and sent in an ad hoc committee to investigate the circumstances surrounding Rider College's issuance of a terminal contract to Professor Daiute for the academic year 1972-73. The bases on which the ad hoc committee took issue with the Rider College administration were: (1) the dismissal of Professor Daiute who under the 1940 statement was de facto tenured (he had been on the Rider faculty ten years beginning the fall of 1970 when he made application for tenure and promotion), and therefore could be dismissed only "for adequate cause and with full academic due process as set forth in the 1958 Statement on Procedural Standards in Faculty Dismissal Proceedings;" and (2) the fact that the proviso delaying implementation of the 1940 statement continued to be the policy of the Elliott administration.[37]

In a procedure which President Elliott has called a "Kangaroo Court," the ad hoc committee conducted its investigation and drafted a report. The report was then submitted to President Elliott. On February 2, 1973, President Elliott with the chairman of the Rider College board of trustees, another member of the board of trustees and Vice-President Dr. Jerry Brown, met with Dr. Kurland, associate general secretary of the AAUP in Washington, D.C. During this meeting the administrators presented their objections to the draft report of the AAUP. And this meeting was followed by correspondence between them resulting in a revised draft of the ad hoc report. President Elliott stated what he considered the central issue:

> We believe that the central issue revolves about the question of local autonomy, and contend that the faculty of an institution, acting jointly with other members of the institution, possess competence to develop and implement a suitable tenure policy which may not be in strict and immediate agreement with the 1940 Statement. The impact of the revised draft denies this competence both as a matter of policy and as a logical consequence.[38]

He indicated further that "publication of the draft text would be prejudicial and harmful to Rider College and to those individuals named and referred to in it."[39]

The administrators continued to be dissatisfied with the AAUP's report, even in its revised form. This dissatisfaction was based on the administrators' perception that the report still contained "grossly inaccurate material" and that the AAUP seemed unwilling "to take into account any of the facts that we had presented or to make any of the corrections which were obviously called for."[40] Because of this perception, the only alternative the administrators saw open to them was to gain an injunction stopping publication of the report.

President Elliott with the approval of the board of trustees sought a preliminary injunction in court to stop the publication of the AAUP report until such time as the alleged inaccuracies and errors could be removed. Early in March 1973 the college administration lost its attempt to gain a preliminary injunction against the AAUP to keep its report from being published. A superior court judge rejected the college's contention that it would be irreparably harmed by publication of the report, but also refused to rule on whether or not an injunction would amount to prior restraint on the association's first amendment right of free speech.[41]

On March 13, 1973, the faculty senate responded by passing the following resolution:

(1) The Rider College Faculty Senate, in the strongest possible terms, reaffirms its position of November 24, 1970, that all persons who now meet the criteria of the 1940 Statement of Principles on Academic Freedom and Tenure of the Association of American Colleges and the American Association of University Professors receive tenure now. (2) The Rider College Faculty Senate reaffirms its actions of February 15, 1972, supporting by a vote of 96 to 0 with 5 abstentions the actions of the five faculty committees which considered and endorsed Professor Daiute for tenure. (3) The Rider College Faculty Senate also reaffirms the following resolutions passed by the Senate on February 15, 1972, some of which have since been incorporated into the Rider College Statutes: Whereas, the Rider College administration has ignored faculty committee recommendations not consonant with its views and has readily accepted recommendations consonant with its own views, in the interest of restoring meaningful faculty governance, be it resolved, that the faculty be primarily responsible for appointments, reappointments, decisions not to reappoint, promotions, the granting of tenure, and dismissal. Be it resolved that the Board of Trustees and president, on matters of faculty status as in other matters where the faculty

31

has primary responsibility, concur with the faculty judgment, except in rare instances and for compelling reasons stated in written detail. (4) The Rider College Senate formally repudiates President Elliott's action in attempting to prevent publishing an AAUP investigatory report by court action which has proven to be an embarrassment to the whole college; furthermore, the faculty deplores the fact that President Elliott did not consult the Faculty Senate or the Faculty Association or the All-College Council before taking this drastic action of bringing this internal matter into the courts for all the public to see. (5) The Rider College Faculty Senate expresses its strongest disapproval of President Elliott's handling of the AAUP investigation involving Professor Daiute. Instead of taking the advice of his faculty, the President is proceeding on collision course that can only bring discredit to Rider College. (6) The Rider College Faculty Senate formally expresses its strongest disapproval of President Elliott's handling of the cases of Professor Calcerano, Gishlick, J. Gorman, Eliason, Snyder, and Fischer, all of whom qualify for tenure according to the 1940 AAUP Statement on tenure and all of whom also received endorsement of all the relevant faculty committees but were denied tenure for no good reason. (7) Since the actions of the Elliott administration have consistently violated the principles of meaningful faculty governance and academic tenure, the faculty of Rider College formally censures the Elliott administration and expresses its lack of confidence in that administration's academic leadership.[42]

This resolution passed by the vote of eighty-four yes, ten no, and six abstentions.

The faculty received a memo from the board of trustees dated March 26, 1973, which read as follows:

We join the administration in being deeply troubled by the resolutions that were passed by the Faculty Senate on March 13. The actions of the college administration have been with the full knowledge and concurrence of the Board. Discussions with faculty leaders will be held by Board members and the President between now and the April 13 Board meeting in a further attempt to resolve matters in the best interests of all concerned.[43]

Evidently not much was worked out, as indicated by two resolutions passed by the Rider College faculty senate May 1, 1973. They read as follows:

The Faculty Senate of Rider College reaffirms its categorical belief in the principle of academic due process as formulated in the 1940 AAUP Statement of Principles on Academic Freedom and Tenure, endorsed by more than 80 professional organizations. We deplore the gross violation of this principle by the Board of Trustees and administration. We censure the Rider College Board of Trustees and administration for this violation. The Faculty Senate further notes that Rider College has been properly censured by the National AAUP for violation of academic due process; that the violation of due process has created on this campus a climate in which the professional competence and moral character of faculty members are fair game for slander and defamation—at public meetings, in the student newspaper, and at meetings of the Board of Trustees itself. The violation of the rights of one faculty member undermines the right of all; therefore, the Faculty Senate affirms that it places no confidence in the capacity of either the Board of Trustees or the administration with regard to preserving a climate of respect for faculty rights and due process at Rider College. As a consequence of the violation of the principles of due process, the Rider College Faculty Senate holds the administration and Board of Trustees responsible for: (1) creating a climate in which the professional careers of faculty members can be subject to public character assassination and trial by the press. (2) making Rider College an object of ridicule in the academic world. (3) causing complete demoralization of the faculty.[44]

and:

The chief executives of any organization must bear ultimate responsibility for the stewardship entrusted to them. This is even more true when they take an active role in policy formation. The actions of President Elliott and Vice President Brown in violation of faculty governance have brought national humiliation to Rider College, culminating in AAUP censure. Under the circumstances, Elliott and Brown must stand or fall on the basis of their policies and their execution of them. The harm that has been done the college is not irreparable, but restoration of the college's reputation before the public and among our academic colleagues cannot occur as long as those who created the crises continue to make and execute policy. Without personal rancor, and in great sorrow it should be necessary to do so, we the faculty of Rider College and Senate assembled, formally request the resignation of Frank Elliott and Jerry Wayne Brown.[45]

It was immediately following the court appearance and in the climate indicated by the resolutions passed by the faculty senate that the successful movement to organize the faculty for collective bargaining took place. However, prior to a description of the organization process, it is important to trace through the other issues which the faculty perceived as giving credibility to their developing interpretation of the administration as authoritarian and not collegial.

Faculty Evaluations

In his first speech before the faculty in 1969, President Elliott indicated his concern about building upon the strengths already existing in the faculty. One way to do this, he suggested, was to place greater emphasis on the faculty, having terminal degrees and being involved in research and publication. While he felt these latter areas were more easily evaluated, he also suggested that evaluation of teaching was necessary in order to improve upon the quality of instruction.[46] It was for the purpose of providing "a more precise means of faculty evaluation, one which will recognize both productivity and good teaching," that President Elliott formed the ad hoc committee on evaluation in the fall of 1969.[47]

In President Elliott's first year, evaluation of faculty served two purposes: (1) in order to make decisions related to reappointment, promotion, and/or tenure; and (2) in order to grant or not grant merit pay increases. Obviously, the first form of evaluation was needed at those stages in the lives of faculty when the decisions indicated were to be made. However, for the second purpose some form of annual evaluation of all faculty members was needed.

In February, 1970, the Rider AAUP chapter issued the following statement which was subsequently endorsed by the faculty senate and forwarded to President Elliott:

> We oppose the method used this year in evaluating faculty in the assignment of merit increases. It assumes that objective, fine gradations can be established in merit. Many judgments appear to have been based upon hearsay and irrelevancies; there has been no documentation of judgments and no policy of negotiation. While we agree that it is possible to establish a faculty member's unsatisfactory performance or distinguished performance objectively, we do not believe that fine gradations of merit can be established by mechanically applying some formula. Nor do we condone, on the other hand, arbitrary judgments about a faculty

member's merit. We therefore recommend that salary increments not be based on merit alone; but instead a scale be established based upon cost of living and years of satisfactory service and rank. Only in extreme cases of unsatisfactory performance or distinguished performance should there be deviations from this scale, and these deviations should be justified by documented judgments made in consultation with department chairmen concerned.[48]

President Elliott responded to the Rider AAUP chapter statement and senate endorsement of same by stating:

Dr. Guimond has already communicated the Senate endorsement of the Chapter's February 18 statement on faculty evaluations. I think it would be a mistake to adopt any policy of this sort until after we have heard from the Ad Hoc Committee on Evaluations. This committee, which has a majority of faculty representation elected by the faculty, has been studying this all year long. I think it would be quite improper to act until after their report has been delivered and heard.[49]

The ad hoc committee on evaluation submitted its report to President Elliott in June, 1970. The faculty senate discussed the report in the fall and passed several resolutions related to faculty evaluations.[50]

RESOLUTION NUMBER 1

Resolved that the Faculty Senate is in agreement with the *principle* expressed by the *ad hoc* Evaluation Committee (2-5-2 Committee) with respect to activities to be valued in a faculty member which is summarized as follows:

The two activities most highly valued in a faculty member are effective teaching and scholarly activity. Also valued in a faculty member are his service to the college community and his services to the larger community. Growth in each of the above areas is also to be valued.

RESOLUTION NUMBER 2

Resolved that the Faculty Senate is in agreement with the *principle* expressed by the *ad hoc* Committee on Evaluation (2-5-2 Committee) with respect to the method of evaluating faculty members which is summarized as follows:

The indicators for measuring the faculty member's value in each of the areas stated in Resolution #1 not be quantified but rather be evaluated through a series of written judgments beginning with the faculty member and proceeding by stated steps to the President and Board of Trustees who will make the final decision. Each faculty member will be fully apprised of all judgments made at each level and will have the right to object to any judgments made at any particular level of command by appealing to the next higher level with the final right to appeal his case to a committee of six faculty members elected by the faculty.

RESOLUTION NUMBER 3

Resolved that the Faculty Senate is in agreement with the *principle* expressed by the *ad hoc* Committee on Evaluation (2-5-2 Committee) with respect to the role to be played by students in the evaluation of faculty which summarized is as follows:

> Students should be permitted to participate in the evaluation process not by an expression of opinion of the faculty member or the course directly but rather through judgments made by the student concerning what has happened to him in the learning process in a particular course. The instructor has the right to accept or reject the judgments made by his students but such judgment should be made available to all parties involved in the evaluation process.

Following this a faculty committee to review evaluation procedures worked through the year (1970-71) without developing a more precise way of measuring quality teaching. President Elliott in his convocation address to the faculty, September 13, 1971, stated:

> Dr. Schwartz, speaking for the Executive Committee of the Faculty Senate, recently requested the administration to supplement the recommendations of the *Ad Hoc* Committee on Evaluation by providing the faculty with a more precise delineation of what should be regarded as good teaching. . . , as a first step toward accomplishing the Executive Committee's request, I have authorized this year's version of last year's Veix Committee (occasionally known by its proper title of Faculty Committee to Review Evaluation Procedures) to hire the consultant recommended by the Veix Committee who would help that committee, Dr. Brown and the Student Committee to develop a suitable student course evaluation form. I have also asked Vice President Brown to work closely with our academic deans and departmental chairmen to see if we can develop more precise guidelines involving perhaps even performance objectives for each faculty member and, wherever possible, each course by which we might better identify and reward good teaching.[51]

36

The consultant, from Educational Testing Service, worked with this committee to develop a course evaluation procedure. While participation by the faculty in the course evaluation process was voluntary at this developmental stage, it could reasonably be projected that once a suitable instrument was developed, every course would be evaluated.

As indicated in a Rider College publication, the course evaluation procedure also became a means of introducing changes into the faculty's approach to teaching, i.e., "This vehicle, which is entirely voluntary, is designed to help concerned faculty evaluate their success in meeting the educational objectives of their course."[52] Meanwhile, other events were taking place which gave credibility to the faculty's concern about annual faculty evaluation over which the faculty has little to say.

In the minutes of the October 2, 1971, faculty senate meeting mention is made of the evaluation of the business school faculty by graduates of the program, carried out by mailed questionnaires. While this survey of graduates was carried out as part of a course project and was never an official college survey, the faculty objected strenuously to its use by the administration in its case against Professor Daiute. Knowledgable faculty members questioned the validity of its findings since only about one-third of those receiving questionnaires returned them. The findings were used by the president before the board of trustees to support his recommendation that Professor Daiute not be granted tenure.[53]

In his convocation address to the faculty, September 8, 1972, President Elliott again stressed the importance of course objectives.

> One of the best ways to establish a sense of community and to improve the academic climate is to make our expectations, both academic and individual, for the members of that community as clear and precise as possible . . .

> For some time, various departments have been moving in the direction of establishing clear-cut performance objectives for their courses. . . . It makes sense that we should define, define clearly, both to ourselves and to our students, precisely what it is that we expect a student to know and to be at the conclusion of a course.[54]

Soon after this convocation address the faculty found in their mailboxes the Faculty Activity Plan (FAP). This plan, had it been implemented, would have established both the substantive and procedural aspects of evaluation. Following the report of the ad hoc committee on evalution, the FAP divided a faculty member's activity into five areas: (1) teaching; (2) scholarly activity; (3) service to Rider community; (4) service to the larger community in terms of results; (5) developmental and personal growth. For each of these areas, each faculty member was to develop a plan (objectives to be accomplished during the academic year) and criteria by which acceptable results could be measured. After a faculty member had drawn up his/her plan, a meeting with the department chairperson would be held.

> If the department chairman and the faculty agree on these proposed goals they are forwarded to the dean with a recommendation for approval. If the faculty member and the department chairman do not agree on the goals as stated they would then have a three-way conference with the dean to resolve the issues involved.[55]

A similar procedure was to operate for the evaluation of results achieved at the end of the academic year.

Immediately a storm of protest arose from the faculty. Resolutions from the faculty senate executive committee, the Liberal Arts and Science Council on Academic Policy (LASCAP), and the executive committee of the Rider chapter of the AAUP were quickly passed.

> The Faculty Senate Executive Committee moves that, in accordance with the Rider College statutes, Article IV, Section 1d, no action, decision or implementation of the recently distributed faculty activity plan be made until it has been properly studied and considered by appropriate faculty committees and the faculty senate.[56]

> LASCAP regards the manner in which the faculty activity plan has been generated as a clear violation of the procedures specified in the 2-5-2 report and of the principle of faculty governance. We, therefore, recommend that it not be implemented until it has been acted upon by those faculty committees charged with these functions.[57]

The AAUP's executive committee resolution was prefaced by a quote from the 1966 AAUP statement on government of colleges and universities.

> Faculty status and related matters are primarily a faculty responsibility; this area includes appointments, reappointment,

38

decisions not to reappoint, promotions, the granting of tenure, and dismissal. The primary responsibility of the faculty for such matters is based upon the fact that its judgment is central to general educational policy. Furthermore, scholars in a particular field or activity have the chief competence for judging the work of their colleagues; in such competence it is implicit that responsibility exists for both adverse and favorable judgments. . . .[58]

The resolution of the AAUP executive committee read:

(1) Whereas the 1966 Statement on Government of Colleges and Universities was endorsed by the Rider College Faculty Senate in May 1971,

(2) Whereas the 1966 Statement on Government of Colleges and Universities was endorsed by the Rider College Board of Trustees and incorporated by them into the College's Statutes in June 1972,

(3) Whereas the faculty activity plan does not provide for any colleague judgments, be it so resolved that no Rider faculty member shall either voluntarily or involuntarily submit a faculty activity plan since such an action would be in violation of the principles of college government which have been adopted by the Rider College Faculty Senate and Trustees, the AAUP, the American Council on Education, and the Association of Governing Boards of Universities and Colleges.[59]

There was also a memo from the committee on instruction to all members of the faculty senate dated October 4, 1972, which read:

Resolved, that prior to any implementation, the faculty activity plan be extensively reviewed, first at departmental level and then at the next meeting of the Faculty Senate. Furthermore, we urge the administration to withhold any implementation until completion of this review.[60]

The president had not seen the unilateral implementation of the faculty activity plan as such a major problem and felt that the faculty had overreacted. An indication of the administration's initial response is contained in a memo sent from the dean of the School of Arts and Sciences to a chairman in that school:

Following our meeting of September 29, I have decided upon the following procedure:

(1) I will relay to the president your sentiments as expressed in your motion as to the procedure and the content of the faculty activity plan.

> (2) I am making available to you sufficient copies of the original
> proposal and respectfully request that you meet with the
> members of your department for discussion and implementa-
> tion. After discussing it, file a written report with me in
> which you express the sentiments of your department. I urge
> you to be as substantive as you can be. I, in turn, will synthe-
> size your reports and present them to the president's
> council.[61]

However, when the administration sensed the unpopularity of the
FAP it withdrew it, as reflected in the memo of October 20, 1972,
from the executive committee of the faculty senate to all members
of the senate. (The faculty senate consisted of all full-time teaching
members of the faculty holding the rank of professor, associate professor, assistant professor, instructor or lecturer, including all department chairmen.) It read as follows:

> President Elliott has informed the executive committee that, in
> accordance with the senate's recent resolution concerning the
> faculty activity plan, he has referred this matter to the 2-5-2
> committee. The plan will not be implemented until it has been
> considered by the 2-5-2 committee and the faculty senate.

The executive committee added:

> The executive committee applauds this action by President
> Elliott. The committee believes that it is a step in the right
> direction to have administration, faculty, and students sit down
> together on this important committee to make recommendations
> that, it is hoped, will be acceptable to all.[62]

Evaluation continued to be an issue. It contributed to the unionization of the faculty and remained unresolved at the time of the
strike.

The basic difference in respect to evaluation is seen by comparing
the respective contract proposals of the parties. The administration
proposals stated:

> 9.3 Evaluations will be made by the department chairperson
> and discussed with individual faculty members, and there-
> after the chairperson's evaluations will be forwarded to the
> dean. In turn, the dean will make an evaluation. If the
> faculty member desires a three-way conference thereafter
> between himself, the department chairperson and the dean,
> it will be arranged. If the faculty member wishes to have
> the Academic Vice President join such conference, that will

40

be arranged. Evaluation files are to be available to the faculty member at his/her request.

9.4 The parties acknowledge that the activities of the classroom are an integral part of the teaching-learning process and constitute a significant aspect of the professional role of the faculty member. Any person holding faculty rank at the college shall have the right to observe any class.[63]

The faculty contract proposal read:

Evaluation shall be initiated by the Department Chairman, who prepares a statement that the Department members examine for modification, acceptance, or rejection. Changes must be approved by a majority vote of departmental members. The majority vote of the department determines the department's evaluation of that individual and Rider's decision as to the reappointment or nonreappointment of that individual. For non-tenured faculty members, this final departmental evaluation will be placed in that individual's personnel file.

In all instances, Departmental Chairmen and departmental members responsible for renewal and nonrenewal of appointments shall act in accordance with the *1971 AAUP Statement on Procedural Standards in the Renewal or Nonrenewal of Faculty Appointments* and the *1964 AAUP Standards for Notice of Nonreappointments.*[64]

In short there was disagreement over the purpose of the evaluation (the faculty wanted evaluation tied to a specific purpose, the administration wanted annual evaluation) and the procedures to be used.

Selection of Administrators

Another aspect of the developing situation at Rider College which gave impetus to the faculty perception that the president was only giving lip service to collegial governance was the appointment of two administrators, the vice president for academic affairs and the Economic Opportunity Program director. The faculty perceived these appointments as having been made unilaterally.

The appointment which caused the most turmoil and which will be discussed here was that of Dr. Jerry Brown, assistant to the president, to the position of vice president for academic affairs. Dr. Brown came to Rider College at the same time as President Elliott, August, 1969. He came as President Elliott's assistant, having been hired by

President Moore, with the approval of President-elect Elliott. He served in this capacity for several months prior to the appointment of a screening committee by President Elliott in March, 1970, to search and screen candidates for the position of vice president for academic affairs. Dr. Brown continued to serve as assistant to the president during the months the committee carried on its meetings until December 2, 1970, when the board of trustees accepted him on President Elliott's recommendation and appointed him to the office of vice president for academic affairs.

The office of vice president for academic affairs had been established only after a Middle States Evaluation Report in 1965 recommended the establishment of such an office. While President Moore did not necessarily agree with this recommendation, he could not entirely ignore it. Even though such an office was created and filled, President Moore continued to make most of the decisions ordinarily associated with the position of vice president for academic affairs. One indication of this was the decision to terminate a professor's contract in the history department without the knowledge or approval of the vice president for academic affairs, even though approval was clearly called for in the Rider College statutes. In fact, when the executive committee of the Rider AAUP chapter questioned Dr. Mullen, vice president for academic affairs, about this termination, he stated:

> That in all previous cases he had concurred in the decision to issue such contracts and in every case notification was given at the same time that the contract was issued. [In this case the letter indicating that the contract for the 1968-69 academic year would be a terminal contract was not received until four months after the regular contract.] He further declared that in this case he had specifically recommended that no terminal notice be sent in regard to the 1968-69 contract.[65]

In the light of this situation when the position of vice president became vacant in the spring of 1969, the faculty wanted to be deeply involved in the process by which the new vice president for academic affairs would be chosen. In fact, at the same time the search was going on for a new president, the faculty senate, in the spring of 1969, established a faculty search and screen committee for the office of vice president for academic affairs. It was not made an official college committee by President Moore, due to the understandable wish of President-elect Elliott to have a part in the selection process. President-elect Elliott did make a commitment at that time that the faculty would be fully involved in the selection process once it was initiated.

Upon assuming office, President Elliott took upon himself the duties of the vice president for academic affairs to find out the details involved in the job and also to wait until he knew the college and its personnel more thoroughly before he initiated the processes that would eventually fill the office.

In March, 1970, President Elliott asked Dean Dertouzos (School of Business) "to serve as chairman of a screening committee to seek out and screen candidates for the Office of Vice President for Academic Affairs . . . ."[66] The committee was made up of the "deans of each school, two faculty members from each of the three day schools and four students from the Council for Academic Affairs."[67]

The issue that clearly upset the faculty was that despite the fact that Dr. Brown's name had been eliminated from the list of names being considered for the position by a vote of the committee on July 1, 1970, Dr. Brown was still appointed by the board of trustees to that office on December 2, 1970. The faculty senate established an ad hoc fact-finding committee "to determine what events transpired and what procedures were employed in the selection of a Vice President for Academic Affairs."[68]

The conclusions of the fact-finding committee are presented below with additional comments for clarification.

1) The President is correct when he states that the *Rider College Statutes* grant to him and to the Board of Trustees the right of appointment. Article II, Section 2, Item C reads:

> The Vice President for Academic Affairs of the College shall be appointed by the President with the approval of the Board of Trustees.

2) Neither the letter nor the spirit of the *Rider College Statutes* was adhered to when the Screening Committee was disbanded. Article IV, Section b, Item 3 reads:

> In any policy decision in an area which concerns faculty, arrangements will be made for consultation with the appropriate faculty body or agency before a final judgment or decision is made upon the policy or its implementation. Areas of concern would include . . . , creation, abolition, and staffing of academic administrative offices above the level of the Deans of the schools of the College.[69]

43

The screening committee was disbanded by a letter from President Elliott to Dean Dertouzos dated December 7, 1970. Prior to this time President Elliott had written to Dean Dertouzos on November 16, 1970, that it was urgent that the committee finish the business by the December 2 meeting of the board of trustees. Included in this letter also were the following points as summarized in the report of the senate ad hoc fact-finding committee:

c) He [President Elliott] was disturbed by rumors floating about campus. One of these is that the vice president "must be someone who will oppose the President." Also, some candidates are being considered who have had no administrative experience.

d) "the president should after proper consultation, and as provided by the Rider College Statutes make that appointment himself."

e) Dr. Jerry W. Brown best meets his [the President's] and the college's needs. Therefore, "I must insist that all candidates be weighed against him."[70]

In responding to the president, the committee indicated, in part: "(1) the screening process established by the committee; (2) the extent of which these screening procedures have been employed to date; (3) the fact that no individual has been informed officially of the suggestion of his name; and (4) the possibility exists that further screening by the committee would eliminate some of the names that remain for consideration."[71]

Between the time of this letter and the appointment of Dr. Brown, three student members of the committee sent letters to the president,

expressing their shock and indignation because of the "impossible deadline" he [President Elliott] had imposed on the committee and because he demanded they use as a standard of judgment a man who "did not have the confidence of the faculty and student body." These students felt they had been used in a "dishonorable manner" after having "made sacrifices of time and money to serve on this committee."[72]

On December 7, 1970, the screening committee met for the last time to have read to them President Elliott's final letter to the committee. This was also the day on which the appointment of Dr. Brown to the office of vice president for academic affairs was announced to the Rider College community. The letter contained the following items:

44

a) It is the responsibility of the President to appoint the vice president.

b) He has compared the credentials of the ten candidates submitted by the committee against those of Dr. Brown. None of them met the college's needs as well as Dr. Brown did.

c) He doubts that the committee would ever have unanimously agreed on any candidate.

d) He acknowledges several communications from three student representatives on the committee and denies the allegations they made.

e) He is disbanding the committee.[73]

One interpretation of these events made by many of the faculty was that Dr. Brown had been President Elliott's choice all along and that he had gone through the motions of setting up a screening committee to demonstrate his commitment to collegiality, fully expecting the screening committee to concur with his choice. However, when the screening committee rejected Dr. Brown's name from further consideration, in part, because they did not perceive he had the experience or had provided evidence of strong academic leadership as assistant to the president, the president reverted to the statement in the statutes giving him, along with the board of trustees, the authority to appoint the vice president for academic affairs. He thereby was perceived as circumventing the collegial process which he had asserted was to figure significantly in decision making under his administration.

President Elliott was aware that this interpretation was being made and rejected it, referring to the memo he had sent early in the search process to a student who was a member of the student academic affairs council of the student government association. In this memo of April 14, 1970, he stated:

> I must remind you that this is a "search and recommend" committee. By Statutes and by sound administrative practice, the final decision rests with me and with the Board of Trustees; therefore I cannot assure you that any appointment will be made in which there has been unanimity, either of the committee as a whole, or by the separate constituencies of that committee.[74]

The president was also aware at this time of the feeling among some members of the Rider community, both students and faculty, that the vice president for academic affairs should not be simply a

45

"yes man" to the president. In fact, some were suggesting that the vice president for academic affairs should even be an adversary to the president. President Elliott took great exception to the suggestion.

Wherever the truth lies in these events, their outcome created great concern among faculty with a strong commitment to the collegial governance system.

Their reason for concern was furthered in the discussion surrounding the proposed changes in the statutes and bylaws, and in a subsequent letter sent to the faculty by the faculty senate executive committee. In the December 8, 1971, faculty senate meeting, a discussion was held regarding the revision to the statutes. The faculty were informed that Articles I and II, dealing with administrative offices and the appointment process, were outside the province of the faculty. The faculty was to concern itself only with Articles III and IV, dealing with the faculty association (all members of the faculty including administrators) and the faculty senate (all members of the faculty excluding administrators).

The discussion quickly centered on changes made in the revisions to the old statutes suggested by the faculty. Based on their experience with the appointment of Dr. Jerry Brown to vice president for academic affairs, the faculty committee defined an elaborate structure for the appointment process in order to insure faculty approval of subsequent appointments of persons to administrative posts which were directly related to academic matters. The board of trustees refused to delegate such authority to the faculty, leaving the authority of the president intact while for the moment removing even the consultative role of the faculty. As a result of the discussion, the motion to approve the statutes was tabled.

In a letter to the faculty from the faculty senate executive committee in February, 1972, concern about the revisions made to the statutes was expressed.

> Our immediate area of concern is your vote on the new statutes. At the May 1971 Senate meeting, you endorsed Articles 3 and 4 as prepared by the Stroh Committee. Subsequently the administration revised them, deleting Appendix C, which specified meaningful faculty involvement in selecting candidates for college wide positions. Recently you were asked to endorse Articles 1 and 2 as prepared by the administration and trustees. These specify no machinery for a faculty role in governance;

they state merely that faculty will be consulted when matters concern them. We feel that as they stand, the statutes are totally unacceptable and recommend that you reject them until Appendix C is restored and until your representatives present a revision of Articles 1 and 2.[75]

The letter continues with the following comment, which gives an indication of the thinking of some of the faculty at this point.

A crucial matter that we feel must be spelled out in the statutes is the faculty's right to have a meaningful say in selection of departmental chairmen. In 1974, most department chairmen's terms will be subject to review. The ramifications of administration-appointed chairmen are many—some readily apparent, others not so obvious: for example, if a faculty undertakes collective bargaining, the National Labor Relations Board will not recognize appointed chairmen as a part of the bargaining unit (as at C.W. Post), but will recognize those selected by their departments (as at Fordham).[76]

The faculty were not successful in changing the statutes to read that department chairpersons would be elected by the full-time faculty of the department. This would appear again as an issue in both setting up the bargaining unit and in negotiations.

The faculty thinking on administrative appointments was expressed in a resolution passed by the faculty senate, February 16, 1972:

Be it resolved that the chairman of a department would be selected either by departmental election or by appointment following consultation with members of the department and of related departments, and that these appointments concur with departmental members' judgments, except in rare instances and for compelling reasons stated in written detail. . . . Be it resolved, that academic deans of the various schools of the college shall be recommended for appointment by their respective schools in consultation with the President and Vice President for Academic Affairs.[77]

Resource Allocation

In the first year of President Elliott's tenure, differences also developed between the faculty and administration over the extent of faculty knowledge of the budget and the degree to which faculty would be involved in allocation decisions. In the spring President Elliott created a priorities committee. In the report of the faculty committee members to the faculty, they indicated the faculty perception of these disagreements. As indicated in the report, the initial disagreement came over the conception of the function of the faculty budget priorities committee:

> The administration conception as expressed by President Elliott was, roughly, that we were representative senate members and thus could express the senate point of view without consulting with the senate. We were to the administration primarily a sounding board, and they felt—at first, at least—(1) no need to supply us with meeting agendas until meeting time; (2) no obligation to apprise us of contemplated expenditures, even major unbudgeted ones, if they had made up their minds to spend; (3) no need to give us any more information about the budget than is available to every other faculty member and student. Committee opinion, though ranging at first from the antithesis of President Elliott's (that we are merely an agency through which the Senate can make its viewpoints known) to a position similar to his, evolved to several agreements: that we should recommend by ear on minor matters but should take major matters to the Senate for consultation; and that it is necessary to have an agenda well in advance of the meetings and to receive information regarding major matters in time to consult with the Senate prior to the committee meeting.[78]

At the same time the president was setting up the priorities committee, the members of the Rider AAUP chapter in their April, 1970, meeting were discussing a report indicating that the college was likely to have a surplus well in excess of $300,000. The AAUP recommended to the administration that a role be assigned to an AAUP committee to determine how the surplus income would be allocated.

The Rider AAUP chapter soon heard from President Elliott who wrote:

> As you know we have already created a committee from the faculty, who will review the budget and help establish priorities. I have asked that committee to make recommendations concerning the allocation of funds over which we do have some discretion. Since that committee already exists, and since it does represent the entire faculty (please do not think that I am suggesting that the AAUP does not), I think it would be better to ask that committee to make recommendations concerning the dispensation of any surplus.[79]

The budget priorities committee reported:

> Differences of opinion rose at the beginning of the school term:
> the academic annex was constructed with the budget surplus
> from the previous school year—a surplus that the AAUP had
> called to the President's attention well before the end of the
> year and had asked for the opportunity to recommend alloca-
> tions for. In denying the AAUP request, President Elliott had
> explained that such recommendations would be the function of
> the senate priorities committee. His subsequent failure to contact
> our committee about the matter was, he explained, because
> Dr. Moore, before retiring had arranged construction—to be paid
> for by whatever funds were available. A committee visit to the
> President in protest didn't gain an acknowledgment of error
> but did gain an agreement to check like matters with the com-
> mittee in the future.[80]

In another matter which concerned the expenditure of unantici-
pated funds, funds returned to the college by HUD, the priorities
committee was assembled. They were told that these:

> funds [were] earmarked. . . for either further construction or
> renovation, or for paying off indebtedness, an obviously
> unfeasible procedure. . . because of this limitation, the committee
> agreed (after two meetings and much testimony by the architect,
> the SAGA representative, the campus developer, and Board
> lawyer) that the money should be spent.[81]

The committee members indicated some misgivings about this, primarily because they were called into session during the summer when
consultation with the faculty senate was not possible and they had
no advance notice of the agenda for the meeting prior to the actual
meeting.

An issue which continued to be one of major importance was also
raised in the first year of this committeee (1970-71).

> President Elliott has explained that the Board of Trustees has
> decreed that the line items of the budget not be shown to faculty
> members (and also acknowledged that he would not reveal them
> if the prerogative to do so rested with him). Our committee
> agrees that intimate knowledge of the budget is not necessary
> for us to make most recommendations (as long as it is understood
> that our recommendations are on the basis of limited knowl-
> edge). We agree that revelation of the line items might result
> in interminable, action-inhibiting debate; but most of us do
> feel that we should be able, when the situation demands, to

request and expect to receive budget information not generally available. We are particularly anxious to avoid giving faculty sanction to matters inimical to faculty interests because we have acted on the basis of limited information. A rubber-stamp Priorities Committee that affords such sanction is obviously less desirable than no committee at all.[82]

The committee ended its report by making the following recommendations to the faculty senate:

Because we are attempting to establish a productive relationship with the administration, we suggest that the Senate communicate something like the following to President Elliott:

It is the Senate understanding that in working with the Budget Priorities Committee you will:

1. send members an agenda along with each meeting notification.

2. notify them well in advance of major budget problems about which you want faculty opinion so that they may check with the Senate.

3. seek committee advice about all contemplated unbudgeted multi-thousand dollar expenditures and about all major expenditures.

4. recognize the right of the committee to call a meeting of administration and faculty committee members to be conducted by the faculty committee chairman.

We also suggest that the budget priorities committee for 1971-72 prepare a tentative priorities list during the summer, coordinate it with the Faculty Welfare, Salary, and Fringe Benefits Committee recommendations (and possibly the Student Priorities Committee priority list), present it to the Faculty Association in September, and then, as amended, to the administration.

Additionally, we recommend that dates by which answers are requested be specified.[83]

Another indication of the situation at Rider College in relation to budgetary matters is seen in a transaction between the president and the faculty AAUP chapter president. The faculty executive committee, the senate budget priorities committee, the faculty welfare committee and the executive committee of the Rider chapter AAUP had unanimously requested that the summer school and evening school salaries be increased. The president in response said "no" and continued:

I am baffled by the request that any increase in summer school and the evening school salaries be raised by an amount in excess of what has already been agreed to by the salary committee. I am baffled because it is not clear to me the extent to which each committee is supposed to be dealing with these issues. Following the first meeting this year of the priorities committee, the faculty representatives refused to rank order a list of priority items on the grounds that they were all of equal importance. This was the first indication of the fact that this committee was proceeding on the assumption that the college has unlimited funds. Another indication of this type of thinking became apparent when toward the end of the second meeting, Dr. Mott proposed an increase in summer school and evening school salaries. This proposal was made after salary discusison with the salary committee had resulted in allocating all the money that had been committed to the faculty salary increase last year in planning the 1972-73 budget. This was not unrealistic based upon past advice since by putting the money in salaries for full time instructors rather than for evening and summer salaries, we were following a priority which we arrived at during discussion and subsequently verified on several occasions with the officers of the senate and of the AAUP in the fall of 1969.

May I first point out that if the college had unlimited funds, there would be no need to establish priorities—thus no need for a priorities committee. The fact that the college does not have unlimited funds is evidenced by a $540,000 deficit suffered last year.

Because the college does not have unlimited funds: because the salary committee, following established precedent, chose to give preference to base contract faculty salaries thus expending all that had been budgeted, I find there are no funds available to grant your request. Your proposal of granting a $25 increase per semester hour to faculty teaching in the evening school and summer school would cost the college roughly an additional $47,000 based upon last year's experience. It would be irresponsible for me to recommend an increase in the anticipated deficit of $155,000 to $202,000 especially when I have been told by the Board of Trustees that I must come to them with a balanced budget. I can see only these alternatives: (1) cut back on the increases we had projected for full time salaries for 1972-73 which you and I both oppose, (2) to cut back on faculty and staff—which I find unacceptable, or (3) increase tuition still further—which I frankly think is unreasonable at this point.

51

Recognizing that at this moment no one knows what is going to be allowed during phase 2 on either the income or the expenditure side and that any decision we arrive at may have to be modified or abandoned, I am willing to discuss the first question with the faculty salary committee. Obviously we must move quickly however, if we are to realize our self-imposed December 15 contract deadline. You realize of course that the faculty senate's request that we allot well in excess of 50 percent of any increase in student fees to educational expenses is being granted. Finally, I have become utterly bewildered by the present faculty committee structure. Should not the priorities committee first rank order items for budgetary consideration? Should not the salary committee then deal with compensation? Should not the salary committee have been the committee to raise the issue of the evening school and summer school salaries? With whom should I be dealing on this question of evening and summer school salaries?[84]

In November, 1972, the faculty senate committee on salary and wage benefits made the following recommendations:

(1) No faculty member adjudged satisfactory in performance should receive less than the mean of Rider faculty salaries for the next lower rank;

(2) No new faculty should be hired at more than the mean within the rank at which they are hired except with the approval of the department chairman within the hiring school;

(3) Any satisfactory faculty member who has served in rank for five years and who is below the rank mean should qualify as a case of inequity.[85]

As a final indication of faculty exasperation with budget and salary matters, the faculty senate on February 20, 1973, passed a resolution by unanimous voice vote which in effect put the senate in agreement with a bargaining relationship vis-à-vis the administration concerning wages and fringe benefits. This resolution asked the administration to accept the spirit of negotiations as the means for reaching agreement rather than presenting the faculty with figures already established and a take-it or leave-it attitude. The resolution also stated that "the faculty must ratify any final agreement" and "that the faculty, collectively and individually, must know what any agreement will mean to them in terms of dollar amount before they vote on whether or not to ratify the agreement."[86]

Summary: Origins

In February and March of 1973 all of these issues came to a peak. In the tenure and promotion and evaluation issues, the faculty were well aware that the AAUP's ad hoc committee had drafted its report on the circumstances surrounding the termination of Professor Daiute. Also they were well aware of the situation of their seven colleagues who had been given conditional terminal contracts. All of these colleagues would have begun their eighth year teaching the next academic year, and all lacked the appropriate terminal degree. Also at this time a new dean was being sought for the school of liberal arts and sciences. The chairman of the liberal arts and sciences committee on academic policy and his committee (with some additions) had been appointed by the president to serve on the search committee. In his letter to Dr. William H. McCarroll, President Elliott, after outlining the duties and qualifications he considered important to this position, stated:

> After careful consideration and consultation with Dr. Brown and others, I have concluded that Dr. Iorio is experienced and qualified for this position. The faculty of the School of Liberal Arts and Sciences has demonstrated its confidence in Dr. Iorio on a number of occasions in the past. I have come to share that esteem and confidence. He has had the advantage of working closely with members of the administrative staff and faculty in representing the School and has done so with ability and integrity. He would make an excellent Dean. After careful consideration I have concluded that unless it is your committee's conclusion that Dr. Iorio should be asked to assume this position we should look outside the College for Dr. DeYoung's successor.[87]

The committee objected to the conclusion of the president that they select either Dr. Iorio or seek someone from outside the college. This was perceived as being in violation of the college statutes and violating the meaningful participation of faculty in the college's decision-making processes. The president, in response, clarified his initial conclusion, indicating that it was his intention to make clear his support of acting dean Iorio, and urged the committee to include other candidates from the college, if they so desired. However, given the existing situation at Rider College, it is unlikely that President Elliott's letter of clarification received much attention.

Finally, the faculty senate had expressed its desire to enter into the spirit of collective bargaining with the administration regarding wages and fringe benefits.

With all of this happening, the catalyst for organization was provided when the president, with the knowledge and approval of the board of trustees but not of the faculty, sought a preliminary injunction against the national AAUP and its local Rider chapter to keep them from publishing their report on the Daiute case.

In court on March 13, the president of the Rider College chapter of the AAUP, Professor Dissinger, found himself in an adversary position (as a defendant) vis-à-vis the president of the college (as plaintiff). For Professor Dissinger, this served as the experience which removed any remaining trace of hope that a collegial decision-making relationship between faculty and administration at Rider College could function. The fact that other early leaders in the collective-bargaining movement were current or past leaders of the senate reinforced the role of that body as well, in the movement.

Following the denial of the administration's petition for an injunction, Professor Dissinger went back to Rider College and sought and gained from the executive committee of the AAUP authority to carry out a card signing campaign. Within an hour of beginning the campaign in his own academic building, Professor Dissinger had signed up thirty of thirty-two faculty members. In a month approximately 70 percent of the faculty had signed cards indicating their desire for an election to determine whether or not the faculty would be represented by a collective bargaining agent and, if so, whom that would be. The response of the faculty indicated that they felt collective bargaining to be the only alternative for effective faculty participation in college decision making in light of the experience with the Rider College administration.

RECOGNITION

After 70 percent of the faculty had signed the cards during the course of a month-long personal campaign, the Rider AAUP chapter president personally delivered the signed cards to the National Labor Relations Board (NLRB) regional office in Newark. Rider College administrators were served notice by the NLRB in early May that the AAUP had filed sufficient signatures to warrant an election in order to determine who would represent the faculty in collective bargaining at Rider College.

Rather than go through the election process, the administration and faculty agreed to a procedure which would treat all faculty alike, those who had already signed cards and those who had not. In a letter sent to all faculty members, those who had already signed a card were given the option of indicating they wanted their initial card to stand or of rescinding their initial card. Those who had not signed a card were given the option of signing or not signing a card. Responses were mailed directly to the American Arbitration Association where the count took place.

During the time when this letter was sent, there was an attempt by someone identifying with the faculty to dissuade it from viewing collective bargaining as a panacea. But apparently the letter had little effect. By mid-July the Rider chapter of the AAUP was certified by the National Labor Relations Board as the collective bargaining agent for the faculty at Rider College.

Included in the bargaining unit were all full-time faculty members, part-time faculty members, and members of the college library staff with a minimum of a master's degree of library sciences or tenure as a member of the library staff, and the athletic staff with a minimum of a bachelor's degree.

Several days of hearings before the NLRB were taken up with arguments concerning the status of department chairpersons. The faculty argued for their inclusion in the unit, while the administration opposed it. Prior to an official decision by the NLRB, the faculty withdrew the question under an agreement with the administration to leave open the status of faculty chairpersons to be settled in the subsequent negotiations.

NEGOTIATIONS

An indication of the nature of the forthcoming negotiations was provided by an exchange of letters between the former president of the Rider AAUP chapter, then president of the faculty senate, and the president of the college.

President Elliott wrote to the president of the faculty senate on July 30, 1973:

> On July 18, 1973, the American Arbitration Association conducted a "card count" of applications for membership in the American Association of University Professors and designations of such Association as collective bargaining agent to ascertain

whether a majority of our faculty members wished to be represented by the AAUP as their exclusive collective bargaining agent. The American Arbitration Association has certified the results of that "ballot" indicating that a majority of our faculty have designated the AAUP as their exclusive collective bargaining agent.

We are informed by our legal counsel that all negotiations with regard to terms and conditions of employment can only be conducted with the designated collective bargaining agent in the future. We are informed that any other course of conduct may be "an unfair labor practice."

In light of the fact that collective bargaining negotiations will commence shortly, we do not believe that we can continue to take part in joint committee meetings which bear directly on "terms and conditions of employment." We are aware that negotiations may result in some conflicts with the present Rider College *Statutes*. However, it is our understanding that such conflicts may be resolved by amendments to the Rider College *Statutes* or reaching agreement subject to amendment or modification of any statute which may be in conflict.

It is a bit difficult to think of many committee activities which do not deal, at least indirectly, with "conditions of employment." On the other hand, there are some items of an ongoing nature which must be dealt with. I am determined that the administration should continue its involvement in committees with the faculty wherever such action is appropriate and legal. At the moment, it would appear probable that administrative involvement in the following committees would not constitute a violation: Admissions Committee, Lectures, Concerts and Cultural Affairs Committee, Library Committee, Student Life Committee, ROTC Advisory Committee, Equal Opportunity Advisory Committee, ISP Committee, Task Force for Community Affairs Committee, Honorary Degrees and Emeritus Status Committee, Judicial Council, Appeals Council, Safety Committee, Graduate Council and Curriculum Committee.

I am prepared to permit administrative involvement in those committees with the understanding that those committees will not discuss matters which might be construed as being contrary to the law. On the other hand, involvement in the following committees would appear to be a violation of law: Scheduling and Freshman Orientation Committee, Budget Priorities Committee, Campus Development Committee, Academic Advising Committee, Evaluation Review Committee, Dismissal and Termination of Tenure Committee, Promotion and Tenure Committee, Faculty Research Committee, Welfare, Salaries and Fringe Benefits Committee, and Affirmative Action Committee. In addition, we will have to study and decide what to do with the following committees: Student Aid Committee, Athletic Council, and the Surdna Professorship Committee.

Therefore, until negotiations for a collective bargaining agreement have been completed, we do not believe it advisable that the college continue to meet with the first and third groups of joint committees to discuss items which may be deemed to be "terms and conditions of employment." We have instructed all members of the administration to refrain from attending such joint committee meetings until further notice.[88]

The president of the faculty senate wrote a letter to all the faculty concerning this letter he had received from the college president. In his letter he stated:

I received a letter from President Elliott dated July 30, 1973, stating the following essentials:

(1) That all terms and conditions of employment may be negotiated in the future only with the designated bargaining agent.

(2) That the administration feels that it cannot continue to take part in joint committee meetings dealing with terms and conditions of employment, and

(3) That administrative involvement in the following committees would be in violation of the law: scheduling and freshman orientation; budget priority; campus development; academic advising; evaluation review; dismissal and termination of tenure; promotion and tenure; faculty research; welfare, salaries, and fringe benefits; and affirmative action committee. This interpretation of the law insofar as it implies that the administration's recognition of the AAUP as bargaining agent invalidates most of the customary practices governing relationships at Rider is unduly restrictive and is not compelled by federal labor law. Accordingly, in order to insure maximum stability as we approach collective bargaining, it is the position of the faculty senate executive committee that the Rider College statutes remain in full effect.

With regard to joint faculty-administrative committees, there is nothing in the law which prohibits such committees from operating as study committees whose findings can be

57

made available to the appropriate negotiating teams for discussion and implementation. To be sure such committees cannot negotiate terms and conditions of employment, but they certainly can recommend policy.

On the role of department chairmen, about which some confusion has been generated, the Statutes and the AAUP are quite clear. Chairmen are faculty members first of all with undisputed eligibility for membership in the AAUP. Furthermore, the AAUP agreed to a card count recognition to preclude a ruling of the National Labor Relations Board excluding department chairmen from the bargaining unit. In short, Rider College chairmen have not been declared managers, supervisors or administrators by the NLRB. Such declarations have been made only by the Rider College administration and do not have the force of law. In any institution claiming to be a college or university, such an industrial model of the functions of chairmen violates the concept of collegiality at the departmental level and is inconsistent with the Rider College statutes, the 1966 Statement on Government of Colleges and Universities endorsed by the Rider College Board of Trustees and so noted in the statutes. In accord with the statutes, therefore, chairmen are not prohibited by law from participating fully in faculty senate affairs.[89]

President Elliott responded to Professor Dissinger (faculty senate president) in a letter (which was also sent to all the faculty) stating:

Surely in your joint role as President of the Faculty Senate and member of the executive committee of the local chapter of the AAUP you cannot be as naive as your letter of September 11, 1973 would make you appear. We are truly disappointed that you have sought to commence a propaganda campaign, rather than enter into collective bargaining on a mutually conciliatory basis, as we have requested. Unfortunately, your recent letter to the faculty is replete with distortions and misleading comments. We have never even suggested that we are abrogating the present statutes and by-laws of the college but advised Mr. Gishlick and the local chapter of the AAUP on September 20, 1973 in writing as follows: 'We are in complete agreement that the present statutes and by-laws continue to govern this college unless and until they are modified and or amended by the Board of Trustees or a collective bargaining agreement.' As a member of the executive committee of the local chapter of the AAUP you must know that we have requested on several occasions that we immediately sit down together at the bargaining table where we believe we can resolve any reasonable differences which may have arisen. In fact, I must quote again from my recent letter to Mr. Gishlick where we stated, 'we are ready and even eager to meet with you to commence resolving any proper items of conflict between us.'

Our stance concerning joint committees is outlined in my letter of July 30 and explained in my letter to Mr. Gishlick of September 20 as follows: 'We are certain that you, AAUP, will have considerable input to all these areas, and terms and conditions of employment and we are concerned lest we be charged with unfair labor practices in bargaining with any other group than AAUP. If you will assure us that no items affecting terms and conditions of employment will be brought up for discussion at any of these committee meetings and that you are specifically requesting that these committee meetings be continued we will reexamine our position.'

However and more to the point we would reiterate and emphasize a position which we have stated in another letter. We do feel that it is inappropriate to continue this collective bargaining by mail and urge you to meet with us across the bargaining table, at which time most of these items will probably be resolved. We are and have been ready and even anxious to meet with you in a mutually conciliatory basis to start working out some of our problems. There is really little purpose in continuing to point out all the inconsistencies in your letter to the faculty. It is indeed most unfortunate that no matter how sincerely or frequently we attempt to resolve problems in a friendly and appropriate way and seek the opportunity to meet with you to resolve any misunderstandings, you reply by mail, distorting our intentions and fanning the flames of conflict. It is with great reluctance that we are sending copies of this letter to all faculty. However, we cannot permit you to create an atmosphere of suspicion and mistrust based upon totally erroneous information. We do not want conflict, but rather conciliation; we are not intransigent but seek reasonable understanding; we are not interested in propaganda but only in a resolution of matters of vital interest to our college and its faculty. Let us once and for all terminate this political climate and get down to sincere discussion at the collective bargaining table. For the third time in a week, we again request that you meet with us at the collective bargaining table.[90]

The negotiating teams for the faculty and administration sat dow at the bargaining table in late September 1973. The first months wer spent airing faculty grievances and discussing problem areas. It wa not until January 1974 that the faculty actually developed and pre sented their contract proposals, a document which contained thirty eight articles and was sixty-eight pages long. The administratio proposal contained eleven articles and was eleven pages long. Th basic thrust of the faculty's proposal was to ensure "effective" facult participation in the governance of the college, spelled out at eac level (department, school and college) and to have an equitable salar schedule. On the other hand, the administration's proposal coul be interpreted as an attempt to maintain wide administrative discretio in decision making.

While progress seemed slow and sporadic during the early month of negotiations and during the summer, the teams did continue to mee and agreement was reached on retrenchment, past practices, and o some aspects of the tenure article.

In August the tempo picked up considerably. Agreement wa reached on twelve articles, including most of the governance issues However, when the academic year began in September, the momen tum was lost and additional agreement was slow in coming. (A gen eral faculty interpretation of this switch was that the administratio feared some kind of faculty job action if the fall semester arrivec without a contract; when the college opened with no incident momentum suffered.)

The minutes of the AAUP meeting, October 1, 1974, summarized a report given by Professor Walther, chief negotiator for the faculty which included the issues still outstanding.[91]

> The administration's willingness to bargain has fluctuated wildly. In June and July, they were very disinterested. With the fall semester approaching, their attitude appeared to change and the August sessions were quite productive. But with the new semester under way and the faculty back and teaching, the administration team again seems unwilling to bargain consci- entiously. Prof. Walther estimates that 3/4 of the requested issues brought to the bargaining table have been agreed upon. However, 5 crucial issues plus some miscellaneous ones remain unresolved:

	AAUP Stand	Administration Stand
1. the status of dept. chair-persons (about 22 people)	wants them included in the bargaining unit	wants them considered part of the adminis. and excluded from the unit. rejects the idea of a chair-person being acctbl. to the faculty in his dept.
2. required annual evaluations	has agreed to the use of evaluations which have operational consequences rejects addtl. required annual evaluations	insists on addtl. evaluations (of ETS-IBM type) though maintaining that they will not be used punitively
3. agency shop — this is the legal provision that all persons receiving the benefits of the bargaining be assessed for the costs involved	seeks this. It would spread AAUP dues payment over the entire bargaining unit membership. This would reduce the dues payments for present members	their lawyer has said he favors this as a fair means of financing the costs of bargaining Nevertheless, the adminis. refuses to agree to it
4. work load — after discussion in many bargaining sessions and after one marathon session of more than 17 hours devoted to this topic	the AAUP continues to insist on reduced work loads through recogn. of the acad. value of such activities as research, publishing, respons. for student indepen. study and education-related student involvement in the wider community Also insists on the necessity of living up to original promises regarding adjustmt. of load for ISP's taught	refuses to move beyond 2 concessions: 1.) a maximum of 24 contact hours in the reg. fall-spring acad. year 2.) a max. of 3 diff. preparations per semester
5. the compensation package	originally requested a pkg. of approx. 22.4% increase (this included inequity adjustments, merit raises, promotion increases, grants, sabbatical funding, and across-the-board by rank raises of 10.9% of base salary.) in an attempt to bargain this was reduced to a pkg. of 16.4% it was further reduced to a pkg. of 13.5%	originally offered across-the-board by rank raises of 6.0% of base salary no movement moved to increase to 6.5%

AAUP Stand	Administration Stand
6. miscellaneous items still unresolved include questions such as retirement age and supplementary pension	has requested an extension of the retirement age from ... to ... also insisted on the implementation of a supplementary pension plan to which the admin. had informally agreed even before bargaining began

Following the report, Professor Walther indicated that the faculty could either cave in, agreeing to the offers made by the administration on these issues, or the AAUP membership could send the team back to negotiations with a show of support for the team's continuing efforts. The response surprised the bargaining team. The following resolution was passed by a vote of eighty-four yes, four no, and three abstentions.

> Be it resolved that the Rider College Chapter of the AAUP authorizes the Executive Committee to call an appropriate job action when in the judgment of the Executive Committee an impasse on the bargaining has been encountered and in their judgment all other avenues of resolving the impasse have been exhausted.[92]

The events of the next two weeks were summarized in a "Summary Report to the AAUP Chapter Members" distributed October 13, 1974.

October 6, Sunday: discussion by executive committee of AAUP of possible job actions with the reluctant admission that the most effective job action in terms of its impact on administration would be a strike.

October 7, Monday: Memo sent to all the faculty indicating the thinking of the AAUP executive committee and announcing a meeting with the AAUP lawyer, Michael Herbert, on October 11, to provide the faculty with the opportunity to ask questions about the legal and financial implications of job actions. A last-hour membership meeting to be held on October 15, at 3:30 P.M., was also announced. At this meeting the negotiating team would do one of three things:

> (1) they would provide a contract for membership consideration, or

(2) they would notify the membership that, though no contract yet existed, an impasse had not been reached and recommended postponement of the strike deadline on a day-to-day basis while negotiations continue, or

(3) they would report that the impasse reached at the preceding negotiation session had not been resolved, in which case the executive committee, acting upon the authority of the chapter's October 1st resolution, would call for a strike.[93]

October 9, Wednesday: Thirty-third bargaining session—no progress.

October 10, Thursday: President Elliott sent letters to all faculty members presenting his view of the bargaining situation.

October 11, Friday: Jack Pearce, Executive Director, N. J. State Board of Mediation, entered the bargaining situation as mediator and spent two and one-half hours with AAUP legal counsel, Michael Herbert, and AAUP chief negotiator, Professor Sandra Walther.

October 11, Friday: Student newspaper headline read "Faculty Strike Appears Imminent." In the article mention was made of the AAUP *Newsletter* which had indicated that if some progress was not made by October 15, 1974, the faculty would consider striking.

In the same issue two other articles, one of these an editorial, indicated that "on the whole, however, the *News* finds itself supporting the faculty in many of their demands." However, the *News* staff looked on the possibility of a strike with deep misgivings. The other article was a comparative review of the salary figures for institutions of higher education in New Jersey. The data used were printed in the June 1973 issue of the *AAUP Bulletin*. The writer of the column concluded with support for the faculty's request for a 13.5 percent increase.[94]

October 11, Friday: Faculty met with legal counsel to discuss job action and legal protection.

October 14, Monday: The mediator met with administration team for two hours in the morning prior to reopening of negotiations. (In his initial meeting with faculty and administration, the mediator apparently sensed a great deal of hostility so he separated the two teams for bilateral negotiations.) Mediation efforts continued all night and into the next day. The faculty team had set a 3:30 P.M. deadline, at which time they intended to report to the faculty members.

The faculty and administration were close to agreement on a wage package (which at this time, did not include an inequity agreement) and also on the relation of the chairperson to the bargaining unit. The AAUP's legal counsel was perceived by some of the faculty negotiating team members as pushing the faculty to settle on this basis. However, there was still a sense among the faculty negotiating team that the latest offers of the administration team would not be acceptable to the faculty. Much discussion took place among the team members with the general feeling being that they still did not have a saleable package to put before the general faculty. One aspect that concerned them very much was the lack of a resolution of the inequities problem. There were apparently two kinds of inequities in the wage paid to Rider faculty: a within-rank inequity and a between-rank inequity. Within-rank inequity referred to those who were in their seventh year in the same rank and whose salary was below the mean for that rank; between-rank inequities referred to persons who were in their seventh year in the same rank and whose salary was below the mean of the next lower rank.

In addition, the faculty reiterated its request for a two-year contract with Blue Cross-Blue Shield implemented in the second year. The administration wanted a three-year contract with Blue Cross-Blue Shield implemented the third year. The faculty were still unhappy with evaluation procedures, basically because some of the evaluations were not tied to specific purposes and the use of evaluation was left to the discretion of the administration. Further, the faculty basically did not perceive the administration as dealing fairly with them in matters left to administrative discretion.

The administration accused the faculty of wanting the strike, based upon what they considered the introduction of new demands by the faculty at a time when both sides were very close to agreement. The faculty had reintroduced some demands not talked about since early in the negotiations.

The faculty, in turn, blamed the administration for failure to agree, based on their perception of the administration's unwillingness to discuss further what the AAUP team still considered open.

The administration, in its perception of being very close to agreement, saw the faculty's continued efforts to negotiate on certain items, as well as the introduction of items that had not been a part of the most recent negotiations, as an effort to take advantage of the perceived momentum for agreement in order to gain some last minute extras. The administration team was very concerned about setting this kind of precedent in their first contract negotiations and refused to grant further concessions.

The faculty team members, on the other hand really did not feel that they had a resolution of the outstanding issues and did not know how the general faculty would respond to the latest administration offer on these issues. They questioned the mediator, asking him if he felt the administration team knew the consequences of refusing to make additional concessions to the AAUP negotiating team. When the mediator indicated that he thought the administration team did know, the faculty team requested that he return to the administration team and make sure they did. The mediator did as they requested and soon came back saying that they did understand the consequences.

With this event, the faculty team decided that they would have their lawyer present the latest offer on the outstanding items to the faculty in a neutral way (the team was neither recommending approval nor rejection). When this was done, the faculty voted overwhelmingly to reject these proposals and to go out on strike.

THE STRIKE

The strike began in pouring rain on October 16, 1974. (See Figure 2 for chronology.) Faculty support of the strike was very strong with only about 14 of 200 faculty crossing the picket lines. Also, 18 of 22 chairpersons honored the picket lines.[95] This level of support remained constant throughout the eight days of the strike.

The signs of the faculty who were on the picket line expressed the major issues: evaluation, whether chairpersons were administration or faculty, agency shop, the wage package, the secrecy of the budget, and basic mistrust of administration action.

The activities of the faculty during the strike consisted of efforts to keep the total faculty informed about each day's events; efforts to make sure the picket lines were maintained and accurate record kept of faculty crossing the lines; contact with other college and university faculty in the state to elicit their physical, moral, and monetary support; contact with the regional and national AAUP offices to keep them informed and also to elicit their support; and meetings of the executive committee to determine their strategy vis-à-vis the administration.

Various means were established to keep the faculty informed and to give them access to correct information. A publication called the "Strikeletter" was distributed; a telephone was installed in strike head-quarters, and strike headquarters itself was very accessible to the campus and continuously open.

Figure 2

Chronology of Rider College Strike

October 1, 1974	Following a report to the faculty on the status of negotiations, Rider AAUP chapter executive committee authorized to call an appropriate job action in the event of an impasse in bargaining.
October 6, 1974	Decision by executive committee that the most effective job action would be a faculty strike.
October 7, 1974	Call for a membership meeting on October 11 with legal counsel to discuss legal and financial implications of a strike.
	Also call for a membership meeting on October 15, 1974 at which time a final report on negotiations would be given and a decision on job action taken.
October 11, 1974	Mediation efforts begin, directed by Jack Pearce, Executive Director, New Jersey State Board of Mediation.
October 15, 1974	Final offer on outstanding issues rejected at last-hour faculty meeting, impasse declared.
October 16, 1974	Faculty on picket lines.
October 18, 1974	Mediator meets with faculty.
October 19 and 20, 1974	President meets with students, discussion centers about contingency plans in the event college is recessed.
October 21, 1974	Mediation efforts begin again in 20-hour session.
October 23, 1974	Final contract agreed to by both teams.
October 24, 1974	Faculty accept final contract offer.

The mediator, who had held the parties subject to call for a meeting, met with the AAUP executive committee on Friday, October 18. Concern also arose among the executive committee members on the same day, that the solidarity of faculty support might be broken if some faculty who stayed out three days began crossing the picket line Monday. A letter was drafted and sent to all nonpicketing members on Saturday and distributed to all picketing members Monday. It read:

Dear Colleague,

On Monday at 10:00 a.m. negotiations will resume under the guidance of state mediator, Jack Pearce. Our current assessment is that the administration will continue to "stonewall" as long as possible because they still do not believe that the faculty has put its professional conscience on the line.

This next week will be critical in convincing the administration and the public that we are firm in our resolve to see this crisis through to a reasonable settlement. We expect that the administration will hope to crack our most important weapon —our solidarity, by mounting various campaigns to undermine our morale. Therefore, as someone who has faced the morale problem for 12 months, let me give you the following advice:

(1) Get enough rest; nothing clouds perspective more than being tired.

(2) When in doubt, or if you hear negative rumors, call a colleague. Two minds are more likely to assess a situation correctly than one. For direct and accurate information call strike headquarters, 896-0561.

(3) Don't forget that this strike is legal. We have protections under the law and can have them enforced in court if necessary.

(4) Don't forget that they *must bargain* with us. They can neither ignore us nor circumvent us.

(5) Don't forget that this strike *is bad for them*. Their reputations are at stake. *We have brought the College to a halt.* Their nerves are on edge and they cannot pretend that this is business-as-usual. They would like to believe that we are on a "three-day lark." They would also like to see us cave in and come back on our knees. *We won't.*[96]

Sandra Walther
Chief Negotiator
AAUP

Faculty and Board of Trustees Involvement

On the first day of the strike the faculty sent an open letter to the board of trustees appealing to them for a meeting between the faculty and the board. The purpose would not be for bargaining but would serve as a meeting of the minds. The faculty were concerned that the board of trustees were getting a distorted picture of what was happening and wanted to check out the board of trustees' information. In addition, they wanted to make sure that the administration's bargaining team really represented the board of trustees.

The meeting was not held. However, an off-the-record meeting between two members of the faculty bargaining team and a member of the board of trustees was held for several hours. During this time of intense talking, the faculty members perceived that: (1) they had communicated faculty concerns, (2) determined how accurate the board's information was, and (3) ascertained that the administration team correctly represented the board-of-trustees' policy statements to the faculty.

Involvement of National AAUP

The national and northeast regional offices of the AAUP had been involved with Rider College administration and faculty previously concerning the Daiute incident. As reported, it was the administration's attempt through the courts to prevent the publication of the AAUP ad hoc committee report that served as the precipitating factor in the organization of the faculty into a collective bargaining unit. Rider chapter AAUP officers were in close contact with national AAUP officials prior to the strike and once the strike was on, national officers were urged to make their presence known. On October 17, the second day of the strike, "two top officials of the American Association of University Professors arrived at the Rider chapter's strike headquarters."[97] Out of meetings with the negotiating team, these officials pledged support for the Rider chapter and promised some financial support. There was considerable delay in the payment of the financial support, causing some hard feelings toward the national office on the part of Rider faculty. The amount promised, $250, was finally received.

Support from other Unions and AAUP Chapters

Rider faculty received support from other AAUP chapters throughout the state, including Princeton, Rutgers, and Fairleigh Dickinson.

Officers of the AFT state council visited Rider as well as did members of the faculty of Trenton State College.

On the picket line other unions, especially drivers making deliveries, were asked to honor the picket line. These requests were met with mixed reactions.

Role of Students

The students had not been inactive during the strike.

October 17: Some students met with faculty to see if there were ways of exchanging support for each other's positions. The students basically wanted faculty support for their insistence on greater student participation on college committees and full disclosure of the budget. The interdormitory council and the interfraternity council pledged support to the faculty. The student government association stated its "official sympathy with the faculty strike."

October 17: Mass march of about 1,000 students on administrative offices, demanding a meeting with board of trustees.

October 19: Selected members of the elected student body leaders met with President Elliott and board of trustees for question and answer session.

October 20: Administration met again with students. Plans were discussed concerning the possible closure of the college.

The president had reports from the dean of students indicating an increasingly high level of anxiety among the students over the uncertainty of their situation. For this reason he began to think along the lines of recessing the college. He met with student leaders again on Sunday, at which time plans were developed by the president to close the college in the event settlement could not be reached soon. One basis for closing the college was the large number of students around with nothing to do. Student anxiety was perceived by administrators as having increased greatly due to the uncertainty of their situation. The administration felt caught between the necessity of closing down the campus and being close to settlement. The decision was made that a statement on closing would come Wednesday afternoon.

THE DYNAMICS OF SETTLEMENT

The mediator resumed efforts to reach agreement beginning Monday morning. Bilateral negotiations continued all day Monday and through the night until five o'clock Tuesday morning.

After resting on Tuesday, mediation efforts began again Wednesday morning. There was some immediate sign that movement was coming. The first issue on which there was agreement was the acceptance of an agency shop which allowed a conscientious objector clause. This meant that all members of the faculty unit, regardless of membership in the AAUP were required to pay dues, with the exception of those who filled out a conscientious objector form. The lawyer for the administration had been sympathetic to this all along,[98] but had met with resistance from the administration. The wording of the agency shop agreement as it appears in the contract is:

ARTICLE XX

AGENCY RIGHTS

1. *Association Security:* The parties recognize that this is an agency shop agreement, and in accordance with such it is understood that each full time unit member who is not a member of AAUP shall, nevertheless, be required to contribute to AAUP as representation costs, an amount equivalent to such dues as are from time to time authorized, levied and collected from the general membership of AAUP. Unit members who are not members of AAUP and who file an affidavit with the college, together with a copy thereof with the AAUP to the effect that such individuals conscientiously object to participation in and support of collective bargaining activities on their behalf, shall be fully exempt from all requirements in this article.

2. *Enforcement:* The parties recognize that the failure of any full time member of the bargaining unit to pay his dues or his representation costs as aforesaid, to AAUP, shall be deemed just and reasonable cause for the termination of such individual's employment. Procedure to be followed in the event of a violation of the requirements of this article shall be as follows:

A. The AAUP shall notify the full time member of the bargaining unit of non-compliance with the terms of this article by certified mail, return receipt requested. Said notice shall state the fact of non-compliance, shall quote the language and terms of this article, and shall advise such individual that a thirty-day period will be afforded for compliance. In addition, such notice shall indicate that failure to effect compliance within such thirty-day period may result in a request being filed with the college by AAUP for the termination of such individual's employment.

70

B. In the event that such full time member of the bargaining unit, after receipt of the aforesaid notice and the expiration of such thirty-day period shall fail to comply with the requirements of this article, the AAUP shall notify the college of such failure, in writing. The college shall then send a letter to such noncomplying full time member of the bargaining unit, terminating his employment. Such termination shall observe the standards of notification for other terminations referred to elsewhere in this agreement. The AAUP agrees to indemnify and hold harmless the college against any and all expense, liability, damage, or loss, including attorney's fees, resulting from a termination under this Article, which termination is found to be wrongful by reason of any action or failure to act by the AAUP.[99]

The next issue on which agreement came was related to compensation. An inequities fund was agreed to for relief of the within-rank inequities. In the final wording of the contract this reads:

3. Prior to the application of the across-the-board increases referred to in Section 1 above, the College agrees to make the following upward adjustments in compensation during the first year of this contract, effective September 1, 1974, for all full-time members of the bargaining unit who have been in their rank for seven (7) years or more and whose base compensation is below the mean for their present rank—an increase of $700.00 or the sum necessary to increase the base compensation to the mean for such present rank, whichever sum shall be less. During the second year of this contract, effective September 1, 1975, an upward pay adjustment shall be made for all full time members of the bargaining unit who, as of that time, have been in their rank for a period of seven (7) years or more and whose base compensation is less than the mean for such rank. Such second year upward adjustment shall be in the amount of $500.00, or the sum necessary to raise such base compensation to the mean for such rank, whichever sum is less.[100]

Then there was agreement on the concept of evaluation which reads as follows:

ARTICLE XVII
EVALUATION

1. All evaluations relating to reappointment of nontenured faculty, professional library and professional athletic staff, promotion, tenure and retention shall be conducted in accordance with the articles on Reappointment, Promotion, Tenure and Retention of Faculty contained in this agreement.

71

2. The College may evaluate the effectiveness and efficiency of the College, its schools and departments, including the library and athletic programs, in accordance with the pertinent provisions of the academic governance procedure provided elsewhere in this agreement.

3. The College and its faculty have a mutual concern and desire to continually seek to maintain and enhance the professional stature of the teaching and the quality of education at Rider College. In order to pursue these mutual objectives, evaluations to improve or develop the professional performances of individual bargaining unit members or other persons engaged in classroom teaching at Rider College shall be undertaken. Such evaluations shall be initiated at the departmental level. Each department shall adopt the procedures for compiling a written evaluation of the individuals in the department. Such written evaluations may include relevant information supplied by the individual and/or other department members. The written evaluation shall be forwarded to the appropriate dean and shall be placed in the individual's personnel file. Upon receipt thereof, appropriate academic administrators within the particular school shall prepare evaluations of such individuals, giving due deference to the written evaluations received from the department. Such evaluations shall also be placed in the individual's personnel file. In the event that the department shall fail to submit the written evaluation called for herein, the appropriate academic administrators may proceed to prepare a written evaluation of such individual, which shall be placed in the individual's personnel file. The individual shall receive copies of all such evaluations from the source of such evaluations and shall be entitled to reply to any such evaluations in writing and have such written reply placed in his personnel file. The individual shall be entitled to an interview with the appropriate academic administrators to discuss any such evaluations prior to the placement of any such evaluations in the personnel file. A request for such an interview must be made in writing to the appropriate academic administrators within ten days of such individual's receipt of the aforesaid evaluation.

4. An evaluation of courses of instruction involving a survey of students enrolled in such courses shall be undertaken in an orderly and professional manner by the appropriate departments. Appropriate revisions of the survey instruments may be accomplished in accordance with the academic governance procedure set forth in this agreement. Until such revisions have been

accomplished, the most recent survey instrument (instrument utilized spring semester, 1974) shall be utilized. The college will tabulate and compile the results and provide these results to the appropriate faculty member.[101]

In the final agreement, department chairpersons were not considered part of the bargaining unit. However, the agreement includes faculty input to the selection of department chairpersons as described below:

ARTICLE XI
DEPARTMENT CHAIRMEN

1. The parties agree to the principle that the faculty within the various academic departments shall play a strong role in the formation and conduct of academic programs within their disciplines. Each department shall be headed by a department chairman appointed or reappointed in the manner prescribed in this article. The parties agree that it is desirable that a candidate for the position of Department Chairman be acceptable to both the Dean of the School in which the department is located and the full time faculty of the department. The parties agree that the Department Chairman is not a member of the bargaining unit; however, such chairman shall be fully recognized as a member of the faculty and entitled to the rights and privileges of such status.

2. A vacancy occurring in a Department Chairman's position for any reason shall be filled as set forth herein.

3. When a vacancy occurs in a Department Chairman's position, the Dean of the School in which the department is located shall convene a meeting of the affected department's full time faculty. The full time faculty shall then provide the Dean with a recommendation or recommendations for a new Chairman, giving their reasons in writing. The Dean shall appoint a new Chairman from among the recommendations, unless the Dean provides the full time faculty with substantive reasons in writing for rejecting such recommendation or recommendations. Upon such rejection, the Dean shall be free to make a recommendation for filling the vacancy, either from within or without the College, provided however that no appointment of a Department Chairman from outside the College shall result in the loss of a bargaining unit position.

4. Upon the Dean's recommendation of a candidate to fill the vacancy from other than the recommendation or recommendations of the full time faculty, such candidate shall be

interviewed and evaluated by such faculty. If the faculty approves of the Dean's recommendation, the candidate shall be appointed by the Dean. If the faculty finds the Dean's recommendation unacceptable, the Dean may either seek another candidate, who will also be reviewed in the manner set forth in this Article, or the Dean may select the candidate he recommended and provide substantive reasons to the affected faculty for doing so.

5. The terms of all chairmen shall be for a term of two years. Terms of present chairmen, however, shall be fulfilled according to the terms of their appointments.[102]

Blue Cross-Blue Shield beginning the second year of a two-year contract was also agreed to. While these various agreements were being reached and momentum was building in the direction of overall agreement, there was still discussion among the faculty bargaining team concerning the quality of the latest agreements. The between-rank inequity was still unsettled (this was resolved on the basis of the mediator's suggestion that there be created an inequity study committee). One member suggested that the college should be involved in initiating and sponsoring a health maintenance organization (again resolved by the creation of a study committee suggested by the mediator). It was in this context of indecision on the part of the faculty team that the mediator informed the team members that if they refused the offer at this point and insisted on further negotiations the president would recess the college indefinitely and continue negotiations without students on campus. The faculty team perceived this as a threat from the administration. However, the mediator had had this information since Monday but he had not been instructed by the administration to tell this to the faculty. On this basis, it is more likely that the use of the information at this point reflects the mediator's realistic appraisal of the situation, namely, that this was the best the faculty could get and that to push for any more would destroy the present momentum for a settlement.

The information swung the weight of decision making to those of the faculty team who felt they had a good offer. And so the decision was made to have the faculty's chief negotiator present the offer with the recommendation that it be approved. There already was scheduled a meeting of the faculty that evening at 8:00 for the purpose of receiving a report on the progress of negotiations. The faculty gathered at Science Hall, Rider College, for this progress report meeting not expecting the team to come to them with a contract offer. Prior to departing for this meeting the team expressed concern that someone might disagree with a particular issue and attempt to submarine the whole contract. Another issue raised was whether the AAUP's constitution allowed for agreement unless the faculty had the full contract read to them. The settlement agreement was worded by the mediator in such a way as to be consistent with the constitution.

Before the faculty team went over to the meeting the two teams met and exchanged greetings. The administration team expressed to the faculty their wishes for a successful ratification meeting.

Professor Walther was the one chosen to present the final contract offer to the faculty. Prior to this presentation, the faculty negotiating team worked together to shape its content. They decided that, consistent with their previous presentations, a full account should be given to the faculty, including the information on recessing the college. This decision almost resulted in Professor Walther not having a chance to present the final contract offer. The information on the prospective recessing of the college was mentioned early in her remarks. The faculty responded with outrage at what it perceived as a threat. It took about an hour to calm things down to the point where the team felt they could present the final contract offer with some assurance that the faculty would be able to hear it on its own merits.

Two factors made the presentation possible (since there was a heated discussion during this time about whether or not to reject the contract on principle, i.e., in view of the president's threatened action): the standing of the faculty team in the eyes of the rest of the faculty ("after all they have done we should at least listen to them") and the statement by one of the known more radical members of the team to the effect that what would be presented represented a pretty good contract. The final contract offer was presented then by Professor Walther and ratified by an 84-10 vote, the vote coming shortly after midnight on October 24. The next morning the faculty were back in class.

In a separate agreement, the administration and the faculty agreed that there would be no reprisals taken against faculty who had gone on strike, including no loss of pay. The faculty agreed to work out a schedule to make up classes missed during the strike, and also that they would not be involved in any reprisals directed toward students who had not supported the strike.

SHORT-RUN IMPACT OF SETTLEMENT

Did the AAUP achieve anything by engaging in the job action? In terms of contractual issues a comparison of the positions before and after the strike appears to indicate that the faculty definitely improved its position vis-à-vis the administration. The items reflecting this are (1) the agency shop article; (2) the within-ranks inequities agreement; (3) the departmental initiative and input in evaluations rather than administration determination of the criteria and process, and a separation of student evaluations from the personnel decision process; and (4) Blue Cross-Blue Shield insurance provided in the second year of a two-year contract. There had been earlier discussions of Blue Cross-Blue Shield. The faculty rejected a plan in favor of a larger increase in base salary. However, in the second year of this negotiated contract, the faculty got both a salary increment, which compares favorably with past increments, plus the implementation of a Blue Cross-Blue Shield program. The settlement on the relation of the chairperson to the bargaining unit is essentially the agreement reached before the strike, namely, that chairpersons are not in the unit. Compared with the description of formal involvement contained in the Rider College bylaws and statutes, there is greater involvement of the faculty in the selection of chairpersons and there is administrative accountability to the faculty in the final selection of department chairpersons.

One effect the strike had, the lasting impact of which will be hard to measure, is the tremendous psychological change among the faculty from a feeling of frustration and powerlessness to a sense of accomplishment and "we did it." Also it was reported that the faculty-administration tension was substantially relieved. But more time is needed to determine whether the complex governance and grievance processes established in the contract will provide permanent ventilation to the perceived needs and frustrations of the faculty.[103]

NOTES

[1] 183 NLRB No. 41, 74 LRRM 1269 (1970).

[2] Edward P. Kelley, Jr., *Special Report # 12*, (Washington, D.C.: Academic Collective Bargaining Information Servce, February, 1975), pp. 7-9. Data on institutions with collective bargaining agents and those institutions in which a no-agent vote took place. U.S. Department of Health, Education, and Welfare, *Education Directory (1972-73): Higher Education* (Washington, D.C.: Government Printing Office, December, 1972), p. xxii. For total four-year public and private institutions of higher education.

[3] The basic background material has been drawn from: Walter Ashley Brower, Jr., *Rider College: The First One Hundred Years* (Trenton, New Jersey, 1965).

[4] *Ibid.*, p. 14.

5 *Ibid.,* p. 21.

6 *Ibid.,* p. 55.

7 *Ibid.,* p. 67.

8 *Ibid.,* p. 109.

9 *Ibid.,* p. 116.

10 *Ibid.,* p. 126.

11 American Association of University Professors, "Academic Freedom and Tenure: Rider College (New Jersey)," *AAUP Bulletin,* (Spring, 1973), p. 93.

12 *Ibid.,* p. 95

13 American Association of University Professors, "Statement on Faculty Participation in Strikes," *AAUP Policy Documents and Reports* (Washington, D.C.; American Association of University Professors, 1973). This statement was endorsed by the Rider College Board of Trustees on April 7, 1972.

14 Letter, Frank N. Elliott to James P. Begin, June 11, 1975, p. 1.

15 *AAUP Bulletin,* p. 93.

16 *Ibid.,* p. 94. (See also pp. 98, 99).

17 Memo, Guy W. Stroh, President, Rider AAUP Chapter to President Moore, October 30, 1967.

18 *American Association of University Professors Post,* Rider College Chapter, Volume 3, No. 2 (mimeographed).

19 *AAUP Bulletin,* p. 94.

20 Frank N. Elliott (speech delivered on the occasion of his first formal meeting with the Rider Faculty Association, September 8, 1969), p. 4 (mimeographed).

21 *Ibid.,* p. 6.

22 See *Directions at Rider College,* January 1973, 1974, 1975 under "Faculty."

23 *AAUP Bulletin,* pp. 96, 99.

24 *Ibid.,* p. 95.

25 *Ibid.,* p. 97.

26 Rider College Faculty Senate, Minutes of Faculty Senate Meeting, February 15, 1972 (mimeographed).

27 Letter, Frank N. Elliott to James P. Begin, June 11, 1975, p. 1.

28 Report of the President, "The State of Rider College in 1970-1971," p. 2.

29 Annual Reports of the Faculty Committees, Academic Year 1970-71, Report of the Committee on Promotion and Tenure (mimeographed).

30 Report of the Committee on Promotion and Tenure, Minutes of the Faculty Senate.

31 Letter, Faculty Senate Executive Committee to all Rider College Faculty, February 1972, (mimeographed) p. 2.

32 Rider College Faculty Senate, Minutes of Faculty Senate Meeting, February 15, 1972 (mimeographed).

33 Letter, Faculty Senate Executive Committee to all Rider College Faculty, February, 1972 (mimeographed), p. 1.

34 *Ibid.,* pp. 3-4.

35 Rider College Faculty Senate, Minutes of Faculty Senate Meeting, December 5, 1972 (mimeographed).

36 *Ibid.,* meeting of March 13, 1973 (mimeographed).

37 *AAUP Bulletin,* p. 99.

38 Letter, Frank N. Elliott to Jordan E. Kurland, February 13, 1973.

39 *Ibid.*

40 Letter, Frank N. Elliott to James P. Begin, June 11, 1975.

41 *New York Times,* March 13, 1973, p. 47.

42 Rider College Faculty Senate, Minutes of Faculty Senate Meeting, March 13, 1973 (mimeographed).

43 Memo, Executive Committee, Rider College Board of Trustees to Rider College Faculty and Administrators, March 26, 1973 (mimeographed).

44 Rider College Faculty Senate, Minutes of Faculty Senate Meeting, May 1, 1973 (mimeographed).

45 *Ibid.*

46 Frank N. Elliott (speech delivered on the occasion of his first formal meeting with the Rider Faculty Association, September 8, 1969) , p. 5 (mimeographed) .

47 *Ibid.*, p. 6.

48 Rider AAUP Chapter, Minutes of Rider AAUP Chapter Meetings, Meeting of February 18, 1970 (mimeographed) .

49 Memo, Frank N. Elliott to Rider AAUP Chapter.

50 Ad Hoc Committee on Evaluation Report, Appended, Fall, 1970 (mimeographed) .

51 Frank N. Elliott (address delivered at the faculty convocation, Monday, September 13, 1971), p. 3.

52 Rider College, *Directions at Rider College,* No. 6 (January, 1974) , p. 2. As reported here, the course evaluation project had been in operation for three years.

53 Interviews with Rider College Faculty.

54 Frank N. Elliott (address delivered at the faculty convocation, September 8, 1972) , p. 6.

55 Rider College, Faculty Activity Plan, p. 3 (mimeographed) .

56 Rider College Faculty Senate, Minutes of Faculty Senate Meeting, October 10, 1972 (mimeographed) .

57 Rider College, Liberal Arts and Science Council on Academic Policy.

58 The Carnegie Commission on Higher Education, Report and Recommendations by the Commission, *Governance of Higher Education. Six Priority Problems* (New York: McGraw-Hill Book Company, 1973) , pp. 212-13.

59 Rider AAUP Chapter, Resolution of the Executive Committee (mimeographed) .

60 Memo, Faculty Senate Committee on Instruction to Rider Faculty, October 4, 1972 (mimeographed) .

61 Memo, Dean of the School of Arts and Sciences to Chairman of a department in that school, September 29, 1972 (mimeographed).

62 Memo, Rider College Faculty Senate Executive Committee to Members of the Faculty Senate, October 20, 1972 (mimeographed) .

63 Rider College, Administration Contract Proposal, p. 9 (mimeographed) .

64 Rider College, Rider AAUP Chapter, Contract Proposal, p. 18 (mimeographed) .

65 Rider College, Faculty Association Faculty News, September 8, 1968 (mimeographed) .

66 Rider College, Report of the Faculty Senate Ad Hoc Fact-Finding Committee, p. 3 (mimeographed) .

67 *Ibid.*, p. 4.

68 *Ibid.*, Appendix A.

69 *Ibid.*, p. 18.

70 *Ibid.*, pp. 10-11.

71 *Ibid.*, p. 11.

72 *Ibid., pp.* 11-12.

73 *Ibid.*, p. 13.

74 *Ibid.*, p. 4.

75 Letter, Rider College Faculty Senate Executive Committee to Faculty Members, February, 1972, p. 2 (mimeographed) .

76 *Ibid.*

77 Rider College Faculty Senate, Minutes of Faculty Senate Meeting, February 16, 1972.

78 Rider College Faculty Association, Reports of the Faculty Committees, academic year 1970-71, Budget Priorities Committee Report (mimeographed) .

79 Letter, President Elliott to Rider AAUP Chapter, May, 1970.

80 Rider College Faculty Association, Reports of the Faculty Committees, academic year 1970-71, Budget Priorities Committee Report (mimeographed) .

81 *Ibid.*

82 *Ibid.*

83 *Ibid.*

84 Memo, President Elliott to President of Rider College Faculty Association, November 8, 1971 (mimeographed).

85 Rider College Faculty Senate, Minutes of Faculty Senate Meeting, November 14, 1972.

86 *Ibid.*, meeting of February 20, 1973.

87 Letter, President Frank N. Elliott to Dr. William H. McCarroll, February 26, 1973.

88 Letter, President Frank N. Elliott to Dr. Mervin Dissinger, July 30, 1973.

89 Letter, President of Rider College Faculty Senate to Rider College Faculty.

90 Letter, President Elliott to Professor Dissinger, President of Rider College Faculty Senate.

91 Rider AAUP Chapter, Minutes of the Rider AAUP Chapter, meeting of October 1, 1974.

92 *Ibid.*

93 Summary Report to AAUP chapter members, Rider Chapter AAUP, October 14, 1974, p. 2.

94 Ted Rodgers, "Faculty Salary not as High as Rumored," *The Rider News,* Friday, October 11, 1974, p. 7.

95 Rider AAUP Chapter, Strikeletter Number 1, October 17, 1974.

96 Letter, Sandra Walther, Chief Negotiator, Rider AAUP Chapter, to Rider College Faculty, October 19, 1974.

97 Rider AAUP Chapter, Strikeletter Number 2, October 18, 1974.

98 Rider AAUP Chapter, Minutes of the Rider AAUP Chapter, Meeting of October 1, 1974.

99 Agreement 1974-1976 between Rider College and the Rider College Chapter of the American Association of University Professors, pp. 40-41.

100 *Ibid.*, p. 58.

101 *Ibid.*, pp. 37-38.

102 *Ibid.*, pp. 18-19.

103 Interviews with Rider College faculty, July 1975. Information gained from follow-up interviews indicates that while the contract does provide clear cut means for enforcing faculty/administrative relationships the basic perception of the faculty is that the administration is failing "to observe either the letter or the spirit of the contract in good faith." The AAUP's "labor counsel, Mr. Howard Simonoff, has identified their current tactics under the contract as classic 'union-busting' tactics." The President also expresses himself on this by saying "I am not quite sure in what way the faculty/administrative tension has been relieved. Substantially, it is different, and there are clearer cut ways in which to resolve differences. In saying I don't know, I really mean that."

Chapter III

THE NEW JERSEY STATE COLLEGE STRIKE

On Monday, November 18, 1974, the faculty at the eight New Jersey state colleges began a ten-day strike (eight working days), the second bargaining strike in history in a public institution and the first in a multi-institutional system. The AFT-led strike affected approximately 3,200 faculty and nonteaching professionals in the bargaining unit and approximately 78,000 full- and part-time students at the eight institutions: Glassboro, Kean, Trenton, Stockton, Jersey City, Ramapo, Paterson, and Montclair. While higher education in New Jersey is coordinated by a statewide Board of Higher Education, the other public institutions in the state were not affected. The faculty at Rutgers University, the New Jersey Institute of Technology, the College of Medicine and Dentistry of New Jersey, and the fifteen community colleges are in separate units.

From several perspectives the calling of a strike by the AFT would appear to raise significant questions.

First, not only have New Jersey courts ruled that public employee strikes are illegal, the AFT agreement which was in effect during the strike also contained a "no strike" provision.[1]

Second, only three negotiating sessions had been held plus two informal sessions with the Public Employment Relations Commission. The impasse procedures provided by New Jersey law (mediation, then fact-finding with recommendations) had not been initiated by either party and the Public Employment Relations Commission at that time could not by law unilaterally initiate the impasse process (subsequent amendments to the law now appear to give PERC that authority). The AFT had requested immediate fact-finding, bypassing the mediation process, but the request was withdrawn before the strike commenced.

Third, the strike occurred during a reopener for salary and fringe benefit improvements which were not scheduled to go into effect until July 1975.

Fourth, the strike occurred before the February 1, 1975, negotiating deadline established in the basic AFT contract negotiated in February 1974.

Fifth, the AFT was striking against a Democratic administration which the AFT had supported during the election campaign and which had made campaign promises to negotiate in good faith with unions representing state employees. Under the leadership of the new administration, the legislature had made important amendments to the bargaining law which were supported by labor. The governor's counsel, Lewis Kaden, had negotiated for the New Jersey State Troopers with the previous Republican administration and had severely criticized that administration's negotiating style. He had intervened in the negotiations for the basic AFT contract in February 1974, and the contract resulting from those negotiations had seemed to represent the change in direction sought by the public unions.

Given the above factors, why did the AFT choose to go on strike?

In the opinion of the AFT leadership, the strike was an unfair labor practice strike; they felt the state was refusing to respond to the AFT's demands in a timely manner. According to the president of the New Jersey Council of State College locals, Marco Lacatena, the state was subjecting the union and its members to "budgeting strangulation" by delaying salary talks until the legislature had already appropriated higher education funds.[2] He preferred to negotiate a settlement in advance of the completion of the budget process. "I can't wait from week to week and then be strapped with a budget I can't do anything with," he said.[3]

Key to the AFT's motivation was its fear that the pattern of past negotiations was being repeated. The state AFT president claimed that "The budget argument (of the state) doesn't hold any water. The state has been doing this for years. It's the same old runaround, and it's time it was broken."[4]

In another newspaper he was quoted as having said: "We were given that song and dance last year about not being able to negotiate because all state funds had been committed to their current state budget. Now we are being told we cannot negotiate because they don't have any more money."[5]

The state officials, on the other hand, claimed that the budget crunch it foresaw was genuine and was derived from the failure of the legislature to pass an income tax bill.

Barry Steiner, the negotiator for the Department of Higher Education, argued, "We have been frank with them and we have been honest with them. We have said we cannot give them an answer because of the state's fiscal position. We've tried to avoid a charade. They gave their word they would not strike. This situation is a little hard to believe."[6]

The director of the Office of Employee Relations, Frank Mason, added, "We're faced with substantial cuts in many programs, and we are trying to find money to keep hospitals open. There has to be a sense of priorities and for a union to strike in the face of all that is simply irresponsible."[7]

As it has turned out, the budget crisis was real. New Jersey, along with many other public jurisdictions, has been faced with severe economic problems. New Jersey's problems have been compounded by a court mandate to refinance public education. As of this writing (July 1975), the budgetary problem persists, awaiting legislative action on the tax package. But the AFT, despite statements by the governor himself that a salary settlement would not be imposed, misread or chose to ignore the severity of the budgetary crisis.

A full understanding of the AFT leadership's motivations is best derived from a discussion of the historical factors which produced their perspectives. A history of the state colleges and the faculty bargaining relationship follows. Figure 3 presents a chronology of major events.

Figure 3

Chronology of State College Negotiations

1968	Passage of New Jersey Public Sector Collective Bargaining Law.
June, 1969	ANJSCF (NJEA) certified as bargaining agent for state college faculty.
February, 1971	First ANJSCF contract signed.
February, 1973	AFT certified as bargaining agent for state college faculty.

February, 1974	First AFT contract signed.
October 9, 1974	Negotiations under wage reopener commence.
November 18, 1974	Strike begins.
November 27, 1974	End of strike.

THE STATE COLLEGE SYSTEM:
HISTORY AND STRUCTURE

The six original New Jersey State Colleges (Trenton, Montclair, Paterson, Kean, Glassboro, and Jersey City) started as normal schools, three having been founded as early as 1855.[8] At varying times the normal schools became state teachers colleges and, in 1958, all six became state colleges when "teachers" was dropped from their titles. In the late fifties the colleges began to broaden their curricula and in the mid-sixties the pace quickened until by the early seventies major shifts in emphasis to liberal arts had taken place. The two new state colleges, Ramapo and Stockton, which opened in 1971, started out as multipurpose institutions.

The opening of these two new colleges was indicative of New Jersey's efforts to expand enrollment opportunities for New Jersey high school graduates. The expansion was directed by the Board of Higher Education and its administrative arm, the Department of Higher Education, which had been established in 1966 to guide the expansion of higher education. New Jersey historically had exported over half of its high school graduates to other states for their college education. For example, in 1963, it was reported that 55 percent of the high school graduates attended college out of state.[9] By 1974 the number of students in the state colleges had multiplied almost three times in a nine-year span.[10] Statewide, over 50 percent of the students were now attending colleges in state.

The rapid expansion and change in mission of the state colleges and other effects of the establishment of the Department of Higher Education created a number of tensions in the state college system which underlie the faculty's quick adoption of the collective bargaining mechanism and the subsequent use of bargaining's ultimate weapon, the strike.

Before the board and Department of Higher Education were established in 1966, the various institutions of higher education in New Jersey had been coordinated by the Department of Education. While Rutgers University and the Newark College of Engineering (now, the New Jersey Institute of Technology) had been only nominally controlled by the department, decisions in the state colleges were highly centralized in this body. At the state colleges all faculty appointments and promotions were reviewed by the Department of Education. Curricula decisions were also centralized. There were no traditional governing bodies in operation. All state college presidents were hired by the department; indeed one president indicated he felt more like a dean, given his limited authority. The absence of discretion in fiscal matters was a particularly sensitive matter to the individual institutions.

In addition, in the state colleges important aspects of the tenure process, such as the probationary period, are statutorily determined. Decisions in respect to salary and other economic benefits were determined beyond local institutions by the Board of Education or by the legislature. Pensions and insurance coverage, for example, are statutorily determined. The absence of funded sabbaticals can be entirely accounted for by the refusal of the executive branch and/or legislature to permit them.

The reorganization of higher education in 1966 which created the Board of Higher Education attempted to decentralize authority to the individual state colleges by creating separate governing boards for each campus. A major purpose of the reorganization was to free public higher education from the public school establishment, and in the case of the state colleges to break the tight circular relationship which existed between the teacher training institutions and the public schools in which the goals and missions of the state colleges were felt to be overly controlled by the public school establishment.[11] The severance of the state colleges from the Commissioner of Education, a move strongly opposed by the commissioner, had a major impact on historical relationships as will be noted in more detail below.

HISTORICAL ROLE OF NEW JERSEY EDUCATION ASSOCIATION: THE ORIGINS OF BARGAINING

Due to the centralized nature of decisions in the state colleges, extensive political effort was required to bring about changes desired by the faculty. The faculties adapted historically to this decision-making environment by engaging in their own political activities. The NJEA in the state colleges initiated the College Salary Committee in the late fifties to lobby for better salaries and fringes. Thus,

84

by the late sixties, the NJEA through its affiliate the Association of New Jersey State College Faculties (ANJSCF) had a substantial history of representing the interests of the state college faculty, and approximately one-third of the faculty were members.

It was out of ANJSCF's role as the "informal" negotiating agent for the faculty that the drive for collective bargaining emerged. One of the basic issues was salary. In 1966 the faculty at Rutgers University through successful lobbying efforts of AAUP and the Rutgers administration were afforded substantial salary increases when the legislature permitted the transfer of capital construction funds to salary accounts. The New Jersey Institute of Technology, then the Newark College of Engineering, was later given the benefit of similar legislation. But legislation which would have allowed the state colleges to do the same was permitted to die in committee. The inability of ANJSCF in informal negotiations with the new board and Department of Higher Education over the next two years to reverse this situation was a major precipitating force for bargaining.

In November 1967 ANJSCF imposed sanctions on the new (September 1967) Board of Higher Education because the board had not been responsive to ANJSCF's efforts to again establish legal salary parity with Rutgers and the New Jersey Institute of Technology. In May 1968 the board did adopt the NJEA's proposed salary guide, but the legislature did not fully fund the guide.

The formation of the new statewide coordinating authority no doubt disrupted traditional ANJSCF relationships with the state. One source indicated that the initial adversary relationship between ANJSCF and the new board and the board's reluctance to bargain informally with ANJSCF on the salary matter was a function of the joint ANJSCF/NJEA opposition to the legislation setting up the new board.[12] However, in 1968 the Faculty Personnel Policies Guide for all state colleges was developed by a board subcommittee with input from ANJSCF, AAUP, and AFT, although ANJSCF had the major effect since it was more persistent. The final guide was derived from a model submitted by ANJSCF. So while there was substantial evidence to indicate that the new board was reluctant to deal with ANJSCF, there was not a complete ignoring of the traditional representational role of ANJSCF.

The key point is that ANJSCF through informal negotiations with the new board was unable to achieve the elimination of what it thought was the discriminatory salary treatment of state college

85

faculty. But given the legislative reactions to state college salary improvements, both before and after the new board was established and despite NJEA lobbying power, there is some reason to believe that the state college faculty may not have fared any better under the previous organizational arrangements.

In any event, the frustration deriving from the inability of ANJSCF to resolve the salary issue was of major importance in developing support for collective bargaining. The continuing attempts of ANJSCF in the first set of negotiations to achieve salary parity tend to confirm this belief. The matter was not put to rest until a statewide job evaluation conducted by an independent organization confirmed the differential salary treatment of the different types of institutions.

The inability of ANJSCF to represent faculty salary interests effectively through informal negotiations between 1966 and 1968 contributed to its decision to seek stronger decision-making mechanisms by developing closer relationships with the NJEA and by strongly supporting the passage of public sector bargaining legislation. In fact, despite efforts of the new chancellor of higher education to have higher education excluded from the legislation (one of the reasons Governor Richard Hughes conditionally vetoed the bill was to exclude higher education at the chancellor's urging), NJEA lobbying forces were of major importance in convincing the legislature to override the governor's veto.

Given this history, it is not surprising that the *first* unit determination decision issued by the Public Employment Relations Commission under the new law (1968) dealt with the state colleges.

Immediately upon passage of the public sector legislation, ANJSCF organized a campaign for certification as the state college bargaining agent. Starting in September 1968 authorization cards were circulated. The nature of the campaign tends to confirm the statewide focus of the problems. The signature drive was not accompanied by a major promotional campaign in terms of special mailings. Most of the literature which was distributed was low key and did not deal in a major way with substantive issues; the faculty were asked to select ANJSCF as the representative for negotiating salaries and working conditions on the basis of its past history of representing the faculty on these matters through informal negotiations and lobbying activities at the state level.

This is not to say, however, that faculty perceptions were not affected in an important way by local problems. To the contrary, there is evidence to indicate that the change in mission of the state colleges was producing a body of faculty more sensitive to faculty participation in decision making. In the past large numbers of state college faculty had come from the public school system. Perhaps as a consequence, the faculty during the teachers college phase were apparently not averse to an autocratic administrative style reflective of their experiences in public education. Faculty peer judgment in appointments and promotions was spotty and, while faculty did participate on some institutional and statewide committees and while there were meetings of the entire faculty at individual campuses, there were no systematic procedures for faculty participation on any of the campuses or on a statewide basis.

A faculty council began operation in 1965-66 at Montclair State College and a Newark State College Faculty Senate (now Kean College) was in the planning stages during the same year and started operations the following year. Faculty senates at the other four campuses started operations in 1968-69.[13] While the formation of the senates occurred about the time higher education was reorganized in 1966, and the new chancellor was reported to have encouraged their formation, the movement toward the faculty governance mechanisms predated the reorganization of higher education and was more likely a function of the change in mission of the state colleges and the kinds and numbers of faculty recruited to fulfill this new mission. As an indication of the change, at one time NJEA counted the vast majority of state college faculty as members, according to various sources in the state. This high level of membership was a consequence of the hiring as faculty of public school teachers who automatically continued membership in the NJEA. However, as the nature of the mission of the state colleges changed and as the size of the faculties grew in response to growing student enrollments (as noted above, enrollment tripled in nine years), the level of NJEA membership became diluted as many new faculty, unrelated to the elementary and secondary educational establishment, did not automatically join.

In any event, the growth in size of faculty and student bodies, the change in the type of faculty hired and the replacement of old-line administrators created pressure on the essentially autocratic administrative systems of the state colleges. Input on a personal, informal basis by individual faculty members or by ANJSCF was in the pro-

87

cess of being replaced by more systematic traditional governance mechanisms when a less traditional form of faculty governance, collective bargaining, interceded.

Another reason that local governance had not developed at an earlier date was the centralized nature of decision making by the Department of Education described earlier. As mentioned at that point, the development of a statewide ANJSCF role was essentially an adaptation to that organizational framework. The disruption of this role by the new board and Department of Higher Education, and the increasing pressure at the local level for increased faculty participation underlie faculty acceptance of collective bargaining. The decentralization of authority intended by the 1966 reorganization of higher education through the development of individual boards of trustees for each college was not timely.

Another impact of the reorganization of higher education on faculty perceptions of collective bargaining which appeared frequently in interviews was made by statements by the chancellor, Ralph Dungan, some before he assumed office, concerning the quality of the faculty and certain faculty personnel policies. It was reported that he commented on the low percentage of faculty in the state colleges with terminal degrees and the effect this had on their ability to be college faculty. He reportedly also indicated that he felt the Ed.D. degree was inappropriate for a liberal arts faculty. His statement concerning his desires to lengthen the three-year tenure probationary period apparently also created tension among the large numbers of new, untenured faculty. It is difficult to assess the impact of these statements since it is not known how many faculty were aware of them. But reactions to the statements appeared frequently enough in interviews to indicate that they had an impact in shaping many faculty perceptions.

Several faculty members indicated that these actions of the chancellor simply reinforced the opposition to the new chancellor which the president of their institution took particular pains to build up among the faculty before the chancellor assumed office. It would not be surprising if this were a more general occurrence since the Commissioner of Education from whose jurisdiction the six state colleges had been removed had strongly opposed the reorganization. He had also appointed the state college presidents. Within a short period of time five of the six presidents retired or resigned; some were replaced by presidents who did not typically come from the primary and secondary education stream. So the opposition of the state college administration to the reorganization is likely to have conditioned the type of response the chancellor received upon his arrival.

RECOGNITION

In November 1968 ANJSCF requested formal recognition from the Board of Higher Education as the exclusive bargaining agent for all the state colleges, claiming that two-thirds of the faculty had signed authorization cards. The board refused voluntary recognition, in part because there were disagreements between the parties over the scope of the bargaining unit. ANJSCF wanted a statewide unit of all six state colleges, no doubt because it felt it could win a statewide election, but also because it perceived the problems were statewide. The board preferred a unit on each campus. The AFT intervened in the election and like the board preferred single campus units.

The PERC hearing officer recommended acceptance of the board's position, primarily on the basis that the purpose of the recent reorganization of higher education was to decentralize decision making to the state colleges by the formation of separate boards of trustees which had not previously existed. However, in his report, the hearing officer suggested: "If an election to determine their [the faculty's] choice of organization indicates identical choices at all colleges, a single unit would be the practical result." PERC adopted the report of the hearing officer and directed the election.[14]

ANJSCF won the election on all six campuses, garnering three-fourths of the total vote. Less than 3 percent of the faculty votes were for the "no union" option. The AAUP did poorly on the three campuses on which it competed, Glassboro, Trenton, and Jersey City. The AFT did somewhat better on the two campuses on which it participated. It forced a run-off election at Jersey City and received approximately 30 percent of the vote at Paterson.[15] ANJSCF was certified as the bargaining agent in June 1969, and since it had won all elections, it formed a coalition of the six units for bargaining purposes, a coalition with which the Board of Higher Education eventually agreed to negotiate. The AFT replaced ANJSCF as the bargaining agent in 1973, as will be discussed in more detail below.

Included in the current bargaining unit are all full-time teaching and/or research faculty, department chairmen, non-managerial administrative staff, librarians, student personnel staff, demonstration teachers, and professional academic support personnel holding faculty rank.

The five years of negotiations in the state colleges preceding the strike were determinative in the formation of the AFT perceptions of events in the fall of 1974.

Compared to agreements in the state colleges of other states, for example, the Pennsylvania state colleges, the range of issues over which agreement has been reached has been less extensive, though the 1974 AFT agreement represented a change in direction. There are several reasons for this. First, as noted above, many benefits such as insurance, pensions, and tenure are legislated, effectively removing them from the bargaining arena except for lobbying activities.

Second, the New Jersey bargaining law was not among the strongest as far as the unions are concerned. There were no administrative unfair labor practice procedures to enforce requirements to bargain in good faith or procedures to determine the scope of negotiations; courts were the only remedy for the enforcement of statutory rights to bargain in good faith. The scope of negotiations was also limited by a provision in the bargaining law which dictated that no provision in the law "shall annul or modify any statute or statutes of the state."[17] Thus, existing education statutes were given a decided advantage where conflicts over negotiability arose, as a subsequent discussion of specific issues will indicate. In addition, the Republican administration of Governor William Cahill opposed and delayed changes in labor legislation which would have strengthened the unions. For example, the governor vetoed a bill in 1972 which would have provided restrictions to unfair labor practices. But under the Democratic administration of Governor Brendan Byrne (1974), amendments to the law have been made providing for enforcement of the restraints on unfair labor practices by PERC and reducing the impact of the phrase quoted above by limiting it to pensions. As a consequence, the scope-of-bargaining question has been reopened.

Finally, the efforts of the Cahill administration to block legislative changes were reflected in the conservative bargaining approach of the Department of Higher Education and the governor's Office of Employee Relations (OER) in respect to state college negotiations. For example, the administration decided not to negotiate binding arbitration under any conditions, and no union was able to achieve it until a new administration, politically and philosophically committed to a different style of negotiations, agreed to permit it, reportedly as part of a campaign promise. An analysis of specific issues illustrates the nature of the negotiating relationship.

Salary Negotiations

An important goal of the first set of state college negotiations which commenced in July 1969 was an attempt to restore salary parity with Rutgers University and NJIT which had been removed two years previously, as noted above. However, the state negotiator, Frank Mason (director of OER), in the fall of 1969, reported that a statewide salary evaluation (the *Hay Study*) was being conducted and that no increases would be considered until the study was complete. Over the course of negotiations, particularly after the governor's Office of Employee Relations was established by executive order in April 1970, the state's role in negotiations was to increase.[18]

The delayed evaluation report was issued in April 1970, and when mediation and fact-finding had not produced an agreement by July, the state unilaterally implemented the Hay recommendations. The faculty association filed a suit in July claiming that the implementation deprived the state college faculty "of their rights to collective negotiations with the Board of Higher Education."[19] The association also alleged that the governor's Office of Employee Relations and its policy body, the Employee Relations Policy Council, were interfering with negotiations between itself and the Board of Higher Education.

The court disagreed. It found that the governor, not the Board of Higher Education, was the public employer, and that the salary improvements could be unilaterally implemented because negotiations were at an impasse and the state, in the absence of a settlement, had the obligation to provide higher education services.[20]

Due to the delays caused by the court action and a turnover in the state administration (from the Democratic administration of Governor Hughes to the Republican administration of Governor Cahill), the first state college agreement was not signed until February 1971, eighteen months after the start of negotiations.

In subsequent years various means were used by the state to communicate salary increases to all state bargaining units, from joint meetings of all bargaining agents at the state level to individual meetings with each agent. But the message was always clear: the increases are not negotiated, they reflect what the budget will bear. Negotiations have always been delayed until the state budget director has completed his work. No union, through mediation, fact-finding, or strike activity, has been able to break the centrally-determined salary package. Deviations from the pattern for the several state bargaining units have not been major ones.

The fact that the salary increases in recent years have been very competitive with other states has not tempered the union leadership which has been for the most part left out of any direct part in the decision-making process. The fact that nonunionized employees got the same increases particularly angered them. No doubt the wage increases were determined with the presence of unions in mind, but they have not, to date, been the direct result of negotiations. The new Byrne administration came into office in 1974 committed to individual, decentralized salary negotiations but plans were frustrated by a budget crisis of major proportions.

In other areas the Department of Higher Education (DHE) continued to promulgate and implement policies which the unions perceived as having implications for negotiable faculty working conditions. A discussion of tenure and outside employment policy changes follows.

Tenure Guidelines and Procedures

One of the initial goals of the DHE was to bring about basic changes in the tenure process at the community and state colleges. Tenure had been provided after three years—the same as in New Jersey elementary and secondary schools. The major aim of the changes was to limit the loss of flexibility caused by the tenuring-in of these institutions. Failing at attempts to enlist NJEA support for such changes, the DHE attempted to bring about unilateral change through legislation. But the NJEA lobby was successful on several occasions in blocking the legislation from coming out of committee.

"In the absence of legislative relief," the DHE took another route and produced a report, in part the result of efforts of a Council of State Colleges Committee, which took the position that "it is necessary to consider internal modifications of policies and practices which will assist in ameliorating the problem [of too many tenured faculty]."[21]

The outcome of the report was the adoption by the Board of Higher Education in September 1972 of resolutions on tenure policies.

Similar resolutions for the county colleges were passed in October. The resolutions stopped short of quotas but required each local governing board to develop a ten-year plan, establish more rigorous review procedures, limit tenure to individuals with terminal degrees (not applicable to county colleges), and establish a periodic evaluation of tenured faculty.

The faculty association (both state and community college organizations) filed a suit claiming, among other things, that the board had unilaterally instituted negotiable working conditions. The court disagreed, however, upholding the authority of the Board of Higher Education to implement tenure policies under education statutes, and ruling that tenure regulations were not mandatory subjects of negotiations.[22]

Before the New Jersey Supreme Court decision was handed down, the chancellor mounted another legislative effort to lengthen the probationary period. This time he was successful. While the NJEA publicly opposed the bill, its lobbying forces at the legislature were not in evidence. The current bargaining agent, the AFT, also opposed the bill, but its lobbying efforts were also apparently not felt by the legislators.[23] The bill provided for a five-year probationary period for state and community college faculty and called for faculty evaluation and career development programs.

The DHE was given the authority to implement the legislation, and it appointed a committee of state and community college administrators to draft the guidelines. This committee subsequently held hearings for the bargaining agents and the institutional governing bodies, the first time broad-based faculty input in the state colleges had been solicited in this manner.

The AFT, which had replaced ANJSCF as the bargaining agent for reasons to be discussed below, opposed these procedures maintaining that many of the issues being dealt with were negotiable. The AFT was ultimately successful in blocking the implementation of the guidelines in the state colleges as a condition of settlement for the negotiations in February 1974. All new guidelines affecting working conditions would not be implemented until a study commission appointed by the governor completed its work. This agreement was worked out by the governor's counsel, Lewis Kaden, in a meeting in New York City with state AFT leaders Marco Lacatena and Robert Bates, a national field representative, but *not* including any OER or DHE officials. Reports in the press[24] that Albert Shanker, a national

AFT vice president at that time, was present at the meeting were subsequently refuted by the participants although the AFT indicated that Mr. Shanker was involved in other ways.[25]

Outside Employment Policy

In February 1973 the Board of Higher Education adopted outside employment guidelines prohibiting outside employment where such work constituted a conflict of interest or where there was a conflict with job responsibilities. Written permission was required and certain limitations on compensation were included. The ANJSCF (state college faculty) and the Association of New Jersey Community College Faculty protested that the policy dealt with negotiable working conditions and, in part, was in conflict with an existing agreement in the state colleges. The New Jersey Supreme Court agreed that the board's guidelines were negotiable "insofar as they embodied additional restrictions on outside employment beyond those which were preexistent."[26]

Turnover of Bargaining Agents

The conservative stance of the state in negotiations had a number of effects. One of the major factors creating the changeover in bargaining agents from ANJSCF to the AFT was the inability of NJEA to produce. Always a minority representative in terms of membership, over a three-year period from 1969 to 1972 its membership further declined over 20 percent, a sign of growing discontent.[27]

Six months into the first set of negotiations, AFT locals at two state colleges petitioned for separate units at Jersey City and Paterson state colleges, the two campuses at which it had support in the original election. A petition for an election was originally filed in November 1970, but hearings and appeals delayed decisions on the unit until October 1972.

At issue was the scope of the unit. In a reversal of positions from the original unit determination when it lacked statewide support, the AFT wanted units at each campus as determined by the Public Employment Relations Commission (PERC) in its original unit decision in 1969, while the state now preferred a statewide unit.[28] ANJSCF also preferred a statewide unit as it had in the first unit determination. The initial unit decision had derived for the most part from attempts under the 1966 legislation establishing the state Board of Higher Education to decentralize authority to the state colleges. Separate boards of trustees were instituted for each college where none had existed before. However, not only was the expected decentralization never realized to the fullest extent, but the hearing officer in the second case accorded ". . . greater weight to the policy control which the Board of Higher Education exercised over the colleges than did the commission in PERC No. 1."[29] Also after PERC No. 1 was issued, PERC had found statewide units appropriate in other state agencies and the hearing officer thought the reasoning was relevant to the state colleges.

Another relevant factor was that when the ANJSCF was elected as the bargaining agent on all six campuses a coalition of all colleges was formed to conduct centralized negotiations. Also, when ANJSCF challenged the growing role of the governor's Office of Employee Relations during negotiations for the first contract, the New Jersey Supreme Court determined that the governor was the public employer of state employees, not the Department of Higher Education or the individual institutions. As a consequence, when the AFT challenged the ANJSCF as the exclusive representative in 1972, the appropriate unit was then found to comprise all eight state colleges (two new colleges had been added by that time). PERC called for an immediate election.

The AFT was certified as the representative of the state college faculty in February 1973, after getting the exact vote needed to unseat ANJSCF (50 percent of the vote, plus one). The closeness of the election and the ability of the AFT to unseat ANJSCF despite the statewide unit indicates the importance of certain events which transpired during the first set of negotiations. First, the librarians, who were members of the bargaining unit, had their faculty status changed in 1970 as a consequence of the Hay job evaluation. Despite active protests, including court action, the librarians were unable to regain faculty status under ANJSCF. The support of AFT by the librarians was no doubt important during the election since they comprised a few hundred votes.

Second, the state and ANJSCF had jointly agreed to incorporate the two new state colleges opened in 1971 (Ramapo and Stockton) into coverage by the ANJSCF contract, even though the initial PERC unit decision had provided for individual units on each campus. This move alienated the faculty at those two institutions against ANJSCF and contributed to the difficulties of ANJSCF in getting faculty from those institutions to observe the election polling places; ANJSCF had to send other representatives. The fact that these colleges were new and started out as multipurpose institutions meant that the faculty did not have any particular loyalty to the NEA-affiliated ANJSCF and made them particularly sensitive to the decision to include them in the unit.

Finally, top ANJSCF leadership had alienated some of its local leaders by delegating decision making to a few people, including William Hayward, the NJEA staff man coordinating NJEA higher education efforts. This centralization of authority and the corresponding insensitivity to local problems which resulted was no doubt a product of the need of the leadership to focus its energies on problems encountered in difficult negotiations at the state level. The continued focus of the ANJSCF on the state level, following past history, took place in a context in which attempts were being made to decentralize authority to the individual institutions. As noted above, the 1966 reorganization of New Jersey higher education had established individual governing boards at each of the state colleges for the first time, and faculty pressure was also increasing for greater participation.

The evidence of a serious rift within the ranks of ANJSCF is indicated by a letter to ANJSCF and NJEA leaders on July 4, 1971, from the presidents of the local associations at Paterson and Montclair. The letter pointed out and protested the lack of autonomy of ANJSCF from NJEA. It recommended "postponement of formal unification with NJEA in September and advised instead a period of observation during which we will evaluate our present affiliation and consider alternative affiliations." The association at Montclair affiliated with the AFT in May 1972, and one of the leaders of that former ANJSCF association subsequently led the AFT strike as president of the AFT state college locals. In addition, those segments of the statewide bargaining unit most actively supporting the strike were the librarians and the bargaining unit members at the two new state colleges.

THE AFT ERA

Negotiations with the AFT commenced in March 1973, and despite the more militant posture of the AFT, negotiations were not concluded until almost a year later, and then only after the AFT employed a strike threat. Much of the delay was caused by the AFT's "getting its act together" and the extremely large number of AFT demands. But, once again, the AFT was confronted with many of the same problems as ANJSCF. Salary negotiations awaited the completion of the budget process and, though the state college faculty got the increase first, all state employees—unionized or not—were eventually afforded the same salary increase of six percent plus scheduled salary increments.

As in the first round of ANJSCF negotiations, a gubernatorial election intervened. In fact, after having failed to reach a settlement after several months of negotiations, the AFT delayed negotiations and the threatened job action until a new Democratic governor, whom labor helped elect and from whom campaign promises had reportedly been received, was in office.

Soon after taking office in 1974, the new Democratic Governor Byrne became involved in the negotiations through his counsel, Lewis Kaden, who, in representing state employees under the previous governor, had sharply criticized the state's style of negotiations. To avert a strike, the governor's counsel met privately with AFT leaders to discuss the problem areas. To the consternation of those officials who had been conducting negotiations for the state, it was clear that they were no longer in control of the negotiations. One member privately said: "We recive our marching orders from [the governor's counsel]." Under pressure from the governor's office the college presidents gave in on some issues. When it became clear that binding arbitration was to be agreed to, the chancellor did request to be consulted on the specifics, particularly possible exclusions. In addition to the agreement for arbitration, a major gain for the union was that all policy changes dealing with working conditions were to be held up until a study commission to resolve the conflict between the collective bargaining law and other state laws submitted a report. Local negotiations on a variety of issues were also agreed to.

So while ANJSCF had fought and lost the battle to keep the state out of negotiations, the AFT quite effectively used political pressure to open up negotiations. In going this route it was duplicating the style of the chancellor who had also bypassed the bargaining process by going directly to the legislature to bring about tenure changes.

However, there was not total faculty support of the agreement. Many faculty were unhappy about being "cranked up" for a strike, having it delayed several times before being called off, and then finding

97

that some of the key issues used to get faculty support for the strike were not resolved. Once again the librarians' status had not been resolved, though one state negotiator indicated they had negotiated the problem until they were "blue in the face." As a consequence, some of the librarian opposed ratification.

Opposition to the salary settlement (6 percent plus increment) arose on several campuses, particularly from the many faculty at the top of their ranges. The absence of a contractual retrenchment procedure, a contractual requirement that reasons for nonreappointment decisions be given, and a retraction of the implementation of the tenure and evaluation policies also caused problems because the AFT had used these issues to build faculty strike support. Nonreappointment decisions under the new contract were grievable (they had not been in the ANJSCF agreement), and were subject to advisory but not binding arbitration as sought by the AFT. The tenure changes were delayed by the establishment of a study commission, but not totally prevented, although as of this writing they have not been implemented.

ANJSCF opposed ratification of the contract, indicating that the faculty could not harm itself financially since all state employees were getting the same increase anyway. Despite the opposition the contract was ratified by a two-to-one margin. However, even the ratification voting procedures were criticized because the AFT did not submit the vote to an independent organization for counting. The AFT countered that when ANJSCF was the bargaining agent only members could ratify the contract whereas AFT opened the vote up to all members of the bargaining unit.

In any event, the contract was not widely embraced by the faculty as a victory, even though the agreement represented a significant change in direction. (It was the first contract governing state employees, for example, which included binding arbitration.) So, the AFT went into the negotiations the following fall less than secure about membership support.

SUMMARY: CAUSES OF STRIKE

The motivation of the AFT leadership in calling a strike the way it did is more understandable in light of the history of negotiations in the state colleges. Frustrations deriving from the conservative negotiating stance of the state contributed to the misreading by the AFT of the severity of the budget crisis. When the state requested that negotiations be delayed until the budget picture was clear, the AFT saw the request as a continuation of the past pattern of state negotiations. As the president of the state college locals said in an interview before the strike, "When the AFT called off the strike in February, 1974, it was at the sincere request of the governor. The governor said he had just taken over and the strike would put him in trouble politically, but if the AFT would not strike, they [the state] would put in a wage reopener and next time we'd have honest negotiations." He continued that despite this promise the state employees are still being "waltzed around and it is the same old State of New Jersey no matter who is governor."[30] The announcement of a budget surplus following the previous negotiations also angered the AFT leadership since they had been told there was no more money.

It is apparent from these comments, and others, that the new governor had lost credibility with the AFT. There was also a feeling that Governor Byrne had undermined or damaged his political power by losing an all-out battle to have an income tax passed by the legislature soon after being elected. Thus, the AFT did not put much faith in the governor's promises to negotiate fairly; indeed, they laughed at his statement. Hindsight indicates that the governor's claims of budgetary crisis were legitimate, and, while subsequent proposals of a legislative study group to close down at least one state college and control enrollment increases at all institutions may have been political tactics to secure passage of a tax, they do underscore the severity of the problem. The president of the AFT locals indicated after the strike that he wished the state had delayed negotiations by being a little less honest, implying perhaps that the nature of the budget crisis did not become believable until later.

Another factor no doubt contributing to the AFT militancy was its need to consolidate constituent support following the less-than-favorable response to the last negotiations. One AFT official in fact admitted that "there were a lot of issues left hanging from the last negotiations."[31] One of the probable forces for settlement in the previous negotiations was the fact that the AFT was subject to challenge by ANJSCF if the contract had not been attained by February 23, 1974, one year after the AFT was certified under PERC regulations. The contract was signed in early February. ANJSCF has always been in the wings waiting for an opportunity to challenge the AFT. At the current time ANJSCF is again trying to build support for a challenge to the AFT. On April 19, 1975, ANJSCF announced publicly what had been obvious for several months—that it was opening a campaign to unseat the AFT.[32]

As far as the timing of the strike was concerned, the AFT timed the strike to give it maximum power in the context of the school year. Fall classes ended before Christmas and the second semester did not begin until February, after the state budgetary process is normally completed. Maximum pressure on the budget process had to be brought to bear in the fall if negotiations were to have any impact on the construction of the budget. In terms of achieving faculty support, the strategy was a successful one. The faculty interviewed on the picket line were extremely concerned about the job security implications of ongoing budget discussions. The chancellor's statement, that in a difficult budget year other state departments should receive higher priority, was also troublesome to them.

But the AFT was not simply facing a recalcitrant state bargaining team, it was facing a genuine budget crisis created by a declining economy and by a legislature reluctant to initiate an income tax.

THE STRIKE

A major difference between the strike at the state colleges and the strike at Rider College is that the state college strike did not occur after lengthy and involved negotiations. The contract signed in February called for a salary and fringe benefit reopener on October 1, 1974. The first negotiating session was held on October 9. (See Figure 4 for strike chronology.) The union was demanding a 21 percent wage increase, a 10 percent adjustment for two ranks, a semi-annual cost of living provision, fully paid family dental insurance, improved medical insurance providing payment for psychiatric visits up to $40 per visit, retirement at 90 percent of the last year's salary, annual cost of living increases for retirees and promotions for 15 percent of the faculty annually. Other open issues as listed on the AFT's request for fact-finding were: travel benefits, job security benefits, sick leave benefits, other leave benefits, holidays, tuition reimbursement, summer salary rates, overload salary rates, and department chairpersons' compensation.

After two additional bargaining sessions (plus two informal sessions with PERC) in which the state claimed it could not bargain until the extent of the budget crisis was known and requested a delay in negotiations until December, the AFT called for a strike vote. Though not officially called in, PERC officials had met informally but to no avail with the parties before the strike vote. It is of interest to note that after an October 23 bargaining session (the third session), the AFT leadership visited Rider College in the midst of that strike and told the AAUP leadership that the state college negotiations were at an impasse with a strike under serious consideration.

Figure 4

Chronology of State College Strike, 1974

October 9	Negotiations on wage reopener commence.
October 16, 23	Additional negotiating sessions.
November 6	Meeting with PERC.
November 8	Strike vote.
November 14	Meeting with PERC.
November 18	Start of strike.
November 20	Meeting with PERC.
November 25	Meeting with PERC.
November 26	Students file suit for injunction.
November 27	End of strike.
December 2	AFT demonstration in the state capitol scheduled. Hearing on student injunction suit scheduled. Reputed date for filing suit for injunction by state.

The strike vote was held on November 8 and the faculty, according to AFT figures, supported the strike by two to one.[33] The administration estimated that only 500 of 3,200 bargaining unit members voted in the election; the AFT would not reveal how many faculty actually voted. A president of one of the college locals did report privately that 223 out of 500 faculty voted at his institution. But the debate was irrelevant since faculty support of the strike did not subsequently prove to be one of the AFT's major problems. What is important is that the AFT, a minority representative, whether its claim of 1,300 members or the state's estimate of 800 was accurate, was able to initiate a strike successfully on this basis.

The weekend before the strike commenced it was reported that the AFT rebuffed further state efforts to set up last-minute meetings to avert the strike. The AFT conceded that the attempts had been made by the state, but argued that there was no sense to meeting since the state was refusing to negotiate a settlement. The AFT was not interested in delaying the strike, particularly since delays in carrying out a strike threat in the spring negotiations had not produced a settlement agreeable to all of the faculty. So the AFT was really not in a good political position to call off the strike. But, more important, the state was unable to give them an excuse to call off the strike; the state could promise nothing until the budget picture was clear later in the year. But at that point the AFT leadership did not believe the severity of the budget crisis.

The strike commenced on November 18 and ended eight working days later with no resolution of the basic contract issues. The AFT was saved the uncertain but probably negative impact of an injunction by the direct intervention of the governor's office. The following discussion of the strike will attempt to sort out the elements of the AFT's failure to achieve all of its objectives.

AFT Strike Organization

Lack of preparation for the strike was not a basic AFT problem. Utilizing the same procedures it had developed for the strike threat in February 1974, the AFT was well prepared. The influence of the national AFT in planning was evident. Strike committees were formed on each campus to generate faculty support. Each campus had a strike headquarters, often at a local union hall. For example, UAW halls were used at Trenton and Ramapo. Telephones were installed. Local government officials were notified of the strike possibility. Instructions were handed out to pickets indicating what they should and should not do and emphasizing that there should be no violence. Loans were arranged by the AFT. The AFT literature solicited student support and indicated that increased faculty wages did not mean tuition increases. At Stockton State College it was reported that the student government association formally agreed to honor picket lines.[34]

Other unions were asked to honor the picket lines through AFL-CIO county councils, and the aid of the state AFL-CIO organization was sought throughout the strike. But few public pronouncements of support came from the other unions, although it is reported they worked silently behind the scenes to put pressure on the governor.

Local union officials on each campus were also quite active before the strike. At Trenton, for example, the local president spoke before the faculty senate and responded to faculty questions. Also on the evening of the first day of the strike, mass meetings were held at all campuses to unify the faculty.

The strike headquarters served as basic sources of information on the local situations, as the linkage to the faculties at the other campuses, and as sources of information to the media. Aside from the information function, the strike headquarters served as the basic rallying points for faculty on the lines; control over the number and distribution of pickets was maintained and efforts were made to supply food and drink. Also kept at strike headquarters were lists of strike breakers. The headquarters also served as orientation points for the state and national AFT officers as they moved from campus to campus to bolster faculty spirit by showing national AFT support.

Administrative Strike Policy

The policy of the administration toward the strike was spelled out by a memo sent to all the faculty from the chancellor's office after the strike vote and prior to the actual start of the strike. The policy was a duplicate of the one developed in response to the February, 1974, AFT strike threat. This memo read:

STATE OF NEW JERSEY
DEPARTMENT OF HIGHER EDUCATION
TRENTON, NEW JERSEY

OFFICE OF THE CHANCELLOR

POLICIES AND PRACTICES TO BE FOLLOWED BY THE
STATE COLLEGES IN THE EVENT OF A FACULTY
STRIKE OR OTHER ILLEGAL JOB ACTION

It has been announced by the Council of New Jersey State College Locals, SFT-AFT, AFL-CIO (herein called the Union) that it will seek to cause a strike at the college on or about November 18, 1974. This action has been announced by the Union despite the fact that it has a fully executed Agreement with the State running through June 30, 1976, containing a com-

103

mitment that there will be no strike during the term of the Agreement. Further, even absent the Union's promise that it would not strike, such conduct by public employees is generally illegal. Participation in any strike or other job action may subject employees to disciplinary action and other penalties in accord with legal action that may be taken. The following statements of State policy are provided to guide you as you make your own decisions regarding your participation in such illegal activities.

1. Each college will operate a system for determining the performance of all employment responsibilities by all members of the negotiating unit during the period of the job action. Employees not present or available for work activities or special assignments will be presumed to be participating in the job action unless such absence is for other cause. Absence for other cause should be reported, where possible, prior to the scheduled activity and on each subsequent day of absence. Where it is not possible to report such absence prior to the scheduled activity, the report shall be made at the earliest possible time. Absence reports including the reasons therefore should be made to supervisors.* Absences must be approved and appropriately documented. In appropriate cases sick leaves must be documented by a physician's certificate.

2. Since not all members of the negotiating unit have scheduled duties each day, participation in a job action will be presumed to commence on the first day of non-participation in scheduled duties, and be inclusive of all days until the first day of commencement of participation in scheduled duties, or until the employee otherwise satisfactorily indicates his or her return to work.

3. The college will not authorize the payment of salary to any employee participating in a job action.

4. The college will remain open for classes and other activities as scheduled so that the rights of all employees to teach and work, and students wishing to learn may be preserved.

5. Students should assume that the responsible teacher will be present at each class session. Should a teacher fail to appear within 15 minutes of the scheduled time, students may presume that that particular class on that particular day only has been cancelled. It would be useful if students would report such cancellations to the dean's office. The College will

* For faculty the "supervisor" is the appropriate dean.

104

make every effort to minimize the impact of any illegal actions upon the student body and it is the College's intent that no student's right to a complete course of study be jeopardized.

6. The college will operate a special information center from 7:00 a.m. to 10:00 p.m. each day during any strike or job action. Its number is 893-4211. Please call this number if you have any questions and particularly if your rights to work or study is being interfered with. By calling this number you may make arrangements to be escorted on and off campus.

The administration of each college did set up procedures for determining which faculty were honoring the picket lines and which faculty were not. No attempts were made to staff classes, as far as could be determined. Basically the procedure used was to send around deans and other administrators to classrooms to determine which classes were meeting and which were not meeting. There were enough administrators making rounds so that no one had more than a few classrooms to observe. Since observation was done toward the end of scheduled class hours, a problem was created for faculty who were crossing the picket line but whose students were not. In order for a faculty member to be counted as present, then, he/she had to stay in an empty room for most of the class period at a place where an administrator could see him/her.

The attendance-taking procedure derived from item 3 of the state policy which stated that the colleges were not to authorize payment to faculty who honored the picket line. This combination (no work, no pay) was perceived by the administration as the basic lever they had with which to get the faculty off the picket line and back into class. As will be seen below it became a hotly contested issue related to the strike settlement.

Faculty Support

Overall, while faculty support was not as overwhelming as at Rider College, it was substantial. As indicated in Figure 5, only one institution had more than 50 percent of its classes meet on the day of greatest faculty support for the strike.

The pattern of faculty support for the strike by campus sustains a conclusion that the strike did not derive from local issues because, if local issues had been an important determinant, then the campus-

Figure 5

Faculty Support of Strike

| | Percentage of Classes Not Met | | |
	11-18-74 (First Day)	11-27-74 (Last Day)	On day of greatest support
Glassboro	50–60	60	65
Jersey City	50	50	50
Kean	50	40	50
Montclair	50–55	50	55–60
Paterson	55	50	70
Ramapo	80	65–70	80–85
Stockton	85–90	80	85–90
Trenton	30–35	15–20	30–35

Source of data: Primarily administrative reporting system; visits to all campuses generally confirmed the methods and attendance levels.

by-campus variation in faculty support could be explained by differences in historical campus relationships. But differences in faculty satisfaction among campuses, as determined by a questionnaire administered a year before the strike (see Figure 6), and the differences in the historical strength of AFT or ANJSCF among the campuses do not generally predict faculty strike support.[35] An answer to another question posed by the questionnaire also appears in Figure 6: Would you strike over salary or work-load issues?

The data in Figure 6 and the actual faculty strike participation are related in the expected direction only for Trenton and Montclair. The faculty at Trenton, which was the lowest supporter of the strike, was traditionally aligned with ANJSCF, was ranked among the highest in terms of the satisfaction dimensions, and was less likely to have indicated a willingness to strike over salary or work-load issues. At Montclair, where around half of the faculty supported the strike, the faculty ranked about in the middle in respect to the satisfaction items and about half had indicated a year before that they would be willing to support a strike over salary and work-load issues. However, given the fact that the president of the state college locals was from Montclair and the fact that some of the initial leadership opposition to ANJSCF came from that campus, greater faculty support might have been expected.

Glassboro, the only other institution to indicate a low disposition to strike, was one of the four campuses showing the greatest degree of faculty support. This institution had also tended traditionally to

Figure 6

Faculty Satisfaction with Selected Working Conditions—Propensity to Strike

Faculty Satisfaction With:	Glassboro %a	Rank	Jersey City %a	Rank	Kean %a	Rank	Montclair %a	Rank	Paterson %a	Rank	Ramapo %a	Rank	Stockton %a	Rank	Trenton %a	Rank
Salary	31.1	3	17.2	6	14.3	8	26.4	4	22.5	5	14.8	7	37.9	1	33.3	2
The operation of promotion and tenure procedures	19.1	5	17.2	6	11.3	8	26.6	3	14.1	7	33.3	2	41.4	1	21.5	4
Participation in decisions regarding institution-wide educational policy	31.1	4	15.6	7	23.1	6	29.2	5	13.0	8	59.2	1	37.9	2	31.5	3
Relationship between the faculty and the central administration	47.2	1	31.2	6	22.1	7	34.1	5	18.3	8	37.0	3	34.4	4	39.6	2
Operations of the Department of Higher Education in relation to your institution	4.1	5	1.6	8	3.9	6	2.1	7	4.4	4	14.8	1	10.7	2	5.4	3
Faculty Propensity to Strike:	%b	Rank	%b	Rank	%b	Rank	%b	Rank	%b	Rank	%b	Rank	%b	Rank	%b	Rank
Should the faculty strike over salary or workload issues?	38.2	8	69.2	1	47.9	5	49.3	4	47.1	6	50.0	3	52.2	2	39.3	7
Rate of Questionnaire Return c	% 44		% 30		% 46		% 47		% 46		% 41		% 48		% 51	
	n=71		n=62		n=75		n=94		n=74		n=26		n=29		n=90	

a Percent of faculty in institution who are satisfied or very satisfied.
b Percent of faculty in institution who indicated yes or probably yes.
c Questionnaire was administered in the Fall of 1973 to a 40 percent sample of faculty.

support ANJSCF. The AFT started from almost zero support when they challenged the ANJSCF in 1973.

The two institutions indicating the greatest degree of faculty satisfaction, including satisfaction with the relationship between their institution and the Department of Higher Education, were the ones with the greatest degree of faculty support—Stockton and Ramapo. The fact that these are the newest institutions (1971) with a generally younger faculty and smaller size (about a third the size of other institutions) probably accounts for the greater degree of faculty support at these institutions. Moreover, the AFT was extremely strong at these institutions. This strength derived in part from the action of ANJSCF when it was the bargaining agent to incorporate these institutions into the ANJSCF contract without local determination.

The lack of faculty support at Jersey City is surprising for several reasons, although the small questionnaire return may have produced an invalid result. The AFT traditionally had a core of members at this institution, which was the only institution in which the faculty forced a runoff election in the 1969 election. Moreover, the institution ranked among the lowest in terms of faculty satisfaction and had the greatest disposition to strike. But the faculty support for the strike fell in the middle range of institutions. One contributing factor may have been the fact that several former ANJSCF leaders were also members of the faculty; it was reported that until ANJSCF supported the strike in the second week, these individuals made a point of crossing the picket line.

At Paterson the degree of faculty support does reflect an adversarial faculty-administration relationship and traditional AFT support, but not a disposition to strike as measured by the questionnaire. At Kean the degree of support reflects the disposition to strike and the absence of either AFT or ANJSCF dominance, but does not reflect a lower degree of faculty satisfaction than the other institutions.

One area of faculty dissatisfaction measured by the questionnaire which all institutions shared was a dissatisfaction with the relationship of their institutions and DHE. These data certainly indicate a faculty disposition to accept AFT leadership claims that the DHE was the villain in the bargaining arena and in budget matters affecting the state colleges.

Data from interviews on each campus during the strike and from the signs of the pickets also confirm that the strike issues were not of a local nature. It was clear from the interviews and the signs that important among the reasons for faculty support of the strike was the job-security implications of the budget hearings which were in progress. In fact, many of the faculty interviewed on the line indicated that if the strike were for wages only, they would not be out there. While it is true that their responses to our questions may simply be rationalizations to indicate that they have broader, more professional motivations, it is clear that the potential impact of the budget was extremely important for the AFT in getting broader faculty support. All the signs at the state colleges were directed against the bad-faith bargaining of the state and potential budget cuts. There were no signs directed at specific complaints against local administrations. Administrators who were also interviewed at each campus agreed with the faculty assessment that issues were statewide and said the strike was really against Chancellor Dungan and DHE. In fact, they appeared somewhat angry because the strike was really not of their doing.

Another statewide issue which was of particular importance to one group of employees who widely supported the strike was the faculty status question for the librarians. At some campuses librarians were among the most active supporters of the strike. In fact, at Trenton State College where the general faculty support was the lowest, two-thirds of the library staff supported the strike. The library issue had been a thorn in the sides of the parties since the job evaluation conducted by the state in 1970 decided that librarians in the state colleges should not have faculty status. In contrast, at Rutgers University the librarians had been permitted to retain faculty status. There is little doubt that the librarians' dissatisfaction with their treatment under this job evaluation not only explained their level of support for the strike, but also explains in large measure the turnover of the bargaining agent from the ANJSCF, under whom they had lost faculty status, to the AFT. Since the AFT received the exact number of votes to win the election, there is some significant support for the position that it was the librarians' dissatisfaction which turned over the bargaining agent.

As the strike proceeded faculty support tended to erode, as indicated in Figure 5. The greatest degree of support at all institutions tended to be during the first few days of the strike. The erosion, though not substantial at most institutions, must have been a definite signal to the union that a lengthy strike would not hold the faculty.

DYNAMICS OF SETTLEMENT

The first effort to settle the strike occurred on November 20 when an informal meeting of the parties with PERC resulted in no progress toward settlement. Publicly AFT justified its refusal to request PERC mediation services officially (it asked for direct fact-finding) on the basis that since PERC was an agency of the state, the AFT could not consider it to be an impartial agency for the purposes of resolving a strike involving state employees.[36]

Three days after the strike commenced the AFT announced that only a full settlement of the strike issues would lead to an end of the strike. Both this statement and the one concerning the unsuitability of PERC were made by a national AFT field representative touring the state college campuses building faculty support.

At the mid-point of the strike, Robert Nielsen, AFT Director of Higher Education, publicly put the full weight of the national union behind the strike. He was quoted as saying: "The whole world is watching the strike in New Jersey. The faculty members who are undecided, the management people who will be dealing with us— they're all watching." Another national official indicated: "We have to show how effective our services can be." At the same time, the AFT announced that the president of AFT, Albert Shanker, was going to be the chief speaker at a rally for the strikers to be held in Trenton on December 2.[37] The efforts of national officials, however, must be viewed primarily as attempts to build local support among the faculty and to indicate to the state that the national backed local actions. The strike itself was generated locally and was not a part of a national organizing campaign. At the final settlement meeting, Robert Bates, the national field representative, was present as was an aide to Albert Shanker. But there were no public statements by national representatives in respect to the effectiveness of the strike.

The success of the AFT in soliciting the support of other unions to honor the picket lines was spotty. But, in general, no campus was crippled by the cutting off of deliveries, although at one institution it was reported that there were no oil or food deliveries or telephone repairs. On other campuses some unions honored the picket lines, some did not. At one campus, for example, the Teamsters did not cross, but construction continued. When asked why they were not honoring the picket line, the construction workers said that they were not supporting the strike because the faculty crossed their picket lines last year when they were on strike. It was also reported that the state was ensuring deliveries by transferring goods to state trucks for delivery to campus.

Token support was also received from other faculty unions in the state. AAUP officers from Rutgers University, the College of Medicine and Dentistry of New Jersey, and Fairleigh Dickinson were noted on the picket lines. The AAUP state conference also sent letters to the governor encouraging him to bargain. Within the state colleges, ANJSCF supported the strike in the second week, but not energetically. One member of the executive board said "the support was voted to show 'solidarity' with striking colleagues, not to demonstrate support for the AFT leadership."[38]

Another tactic employed by the AFT early in the strike was a demand that the campuses be closed down to prevent further violence although generally the picketing at the institutions was not acrimonious. There were isolated incidents of violence at some campuses, but generally people were allowed to pass, shouted at, called scabs and slowed, but otherwise were unobstructed. At William Paterson College two faculty members were arrested by Wayne police after they sat down at one of the campus gates. At Trenton State two students were arrested; one for interfering with a police officer and a second for interfering with the police officer making the arrest. Also at Trenton, a Trenton State College professor jumped on the hood of a student's car and put his fist through the windshield after the student had allegedly attempted to run over the teacher. At Ramapo a picket jumped on the hood of a car crossing the line, the driver raced a short distance and stopped, the picket ripped off the windshield wiper and ran.

For the most part the students were more militant than the faculty in the lines, and they appeared to be involved in many of the incidents which were reported. There were also some incidents in which students were claimed to have hit pickets (at Trenton State, for example).

On most campuses the relationship between the administration and pickets was good. Where there were deviations they appear to have been related to historical relationships between the AFT leadership on campus and the administration (for example, at Trenton State College). It does not appear from the review of the incidents, however, that there was enough violence or potential for violence at any campus to warrant closing the campuses.

Role of Students

On the same day that the parties were meeting with PERC (November 20), students from the state colleges picketed the State House in Trenton where representatives of striking faculty members were meeting inside with the state officials. It was reported that ". . . about 250 students from most of the state colleges marched and chanted in front of the State House today, demanding the resumption of negotiations between the teachers and the state and the reopening of their classes." The student demonstration was sponsored by members of the New Jersey Student Association of State Colleges which is a statewide organization of student government associations of individual institutions. The students claimed that it was a nonpartisan demonstration aimed primarily at getting classes back in session. As one student indicated, "our No. 1 concern is to get our education."[39]

The students were quite active throughout the course of the strike and toward the end created pressure for settlement by their actions.

There was no systematic evidence collected as to the percentage of students who continued to attend class. But there is a general feeling that student attendance eroded considerably over the period of the strike, due in part to the fact that they tired of coming to campus and finding only a few of their classes meeting.

On all campuses some of the students participated in picketing duties. Indeed, they tended to be more militant in their behavior than most of the faculty who were, with a few exceptions, content to quietly walk the picket lines. Students at some campuses often outnumbered the faculty on the lines.

However, student support of the strike was certainly not generalized, even at the beginning. At seven institutions for which information was obtained, one student government association was neutral, four were against the strike, and two voted to support the strike. None of the seven student newspapers for which information was obtained was supportive of the strike.

The diversity of opinion of the local student government associations prevented the formation of a statewide position. One effort at a statewide meeting failed to engender student support for or against the strike. The major outcome of the meeting was that the students should support that side of the bargaining table which met their needs. Kean College did not participate in that meeting, criticizing the statewide organization for its inaction.

On November 26 the Kean College student government association filed suit in Superior Court seeking a preliminary injunction ordering striking faculty members back to work. This was the first legal action brought since the work stoppage began. When filing the injunction at Kean College, the president of the Kean College student organization indicated that "We felt that court action was the only way we, as educational consumers, had to bring this strike completely to an end." He added that the organization might seek a refund in tuition for the students who missed classes during the dispute. The judge set the hearing for December 2, 1974, the scheduled date for the AFT demonstration in Trenton.[40]

Earlier in the strike students at Trenton had also explored the injunction possibility, and it was reported that student organizations at Montclair and Glassboro had either hired attorneys or had otherwise indicated an intention to seek an injunction.[41] In addition to the injunction movement, there were other signs of student activity. For example, at Montclair State College the students, calling themselves neutral injured parties, indicated that if negotiations to end the walkout were not underway by the time they returned from Thanksgiving, they would occupy the student center at Montclair and hold it until negotiations began. This move was supported by the local student government association.[42]

By the end of the strike it appeared as if the student leadership on many campuses was an independent force for settlement derived out of a concern for losing a semester's work.

Administrative Activities

The state had not been inactive in presenting its case. Chancellor Dungan met with student editors before the strike, just as the AFT had courted the students by pointing out in its literature that salaries could be increased without necessarily raising tuition and that the federation was opposed to any tuition increase.

Dungan also had a meeting during the course of the strike with the student government leaders, a meeting about which he was criticized by one of the state college presidents for having said that if he were a student he would stay home and study.

Early in the strike (November 20), Dungan also released a lengthy memorandum indicating that faculty members at state colleges earned more than their colleagues at private schools in the state, including Princeton University, except for the full-professor rank. Dungan in his memorandum indicated "While the facts speak for themselves, they are even more dramatic when one considers that to satisfy these wage demands would require new revenues which, if New Jersey follows past practice, will come from low and middle income taxpayers."[43] The union denounced the chancellor's tactics as "boss tactics."

Throughout the strike the state remained firm in its position that it did not have sufficient information on its financial situation to permit it to negotiate economics. The day after the informal PERC session (November 21, 1974), Governor Byrne in a letter to Marco Lacatena, president of the state college locals, promised that no salary settlement would be unilaterally imposed on the AFT. The governor said:

> I am greatly distressed that the strike of the State College Faculties continues in the face of the no-strike pledge of the Contract. I urge you and your colleagues in the interest of the students to return to your duties immediately.
>
> You have already been thoroughly briefed on the difficult fiscal situation which the State faces and you are aware of the high unemployment in the State and throughout the Nation. We recognize that the effects of inflation are felt by all sectors of the population, including State College Faculty, but a response to wage demands in the public sector must be balanced against the public's willingness to pay through taxes and the equities involved in the wage demands. This administration and I reiterate pledges which have already been made to you that no unilateral decisions will be made in the matter of salaries. They will be negotiated and amendments in the budget will be made as appropriate to accommodate negotiated wage settlements made subsequent to the submission of the budget.
>
> In the light of these assurances, the fact that the present Contract does not expire until July 1975, the fact that the Union is in violation of its Contract with the State, I strongly suggest that an immediate return to work is the proper course to be followed.

On the same day the senate took notice of the strike by issuing a resolution. The resolution is as follows:

> WHEREAS: Professors employed at the colleges and universities of the State of New Jersey are presently engaged in an illegal strike, and

WHEREAS: That strike is proving to be detrimental to the education of the students of the State, in whose interest and for all of our benefits those colleges and universities exist, and

WHEREAS: Those striking professors are presently governed by the terms and conditions of a previously negotiated Contract; now, therefore, be it

RESOLVED BY THE SENATE OF THE STATE OF NEW JERSEY:

That this Senate deplores that strike and hereby calls upon those striking professors at State colleges to return forthwith to their employment duties and to honor the terms and conditions previously negotiated and agreed upon between themselves and the New Jersey State Department of Higher Education.

THE SETTLEMENT

On November 25 a second meeting was held with PERC and, while agreement was not reached, the first discussion of back wages for time lost during the strike took place. Also under discussion at this meeting was the question of who would mediate the dispute. One observer indicated that the emphasis on these issues was a sign that the AFT saw no resolution to the contract issues for which it struck.

On the same day (November 25), the senate passed another resolution "calling on state Attorney General William F. Hyland to 'take any legal action necessary' to end the eight-day-old strike on the grounds that it was illegal under the state constitution for public employees to strike." The resolution was passed by a vote of 20 to 9. Despite this resolution the counsel to the governor said there would be no immediate call for legal sanction against the week-old state college teachers' strike, but said the possibility to take legal action against the striking teachers was still being "evaluated."[44]

From the beginning the state had been reluctant to seek an injunction. State officials indicated that they would rather not seek a court action since that might stiffen the union's position. " 'I think the union would like to see us get an injunction and start putting people in jail,' said one state official. 'But that's not the way that we want to go.' "[45] Marco Lacatena, the AFT president, supported this belief of the state officials by saying that if he were the subject for the court order, ". . . in the finest tradition of American labor I will remain on strike and I believe my people will, too."[46] At a later

115

point in the strike, in fact one day before the strike was resolved, Mr. Lacatena repeated his statement. "My inclination is to be guided by the practice in past labor movements, which is usually to stand up for one's constitutional rights as a union seeking a resolution to a dispute," he said. The past practice to which he was alluding has usually been to ignore court injunctions.[47]

However, as the strike wore on pressure for an injunction from both the students and some officials in the state grew. In response to information that the national AFT had started to assume control of the strike, Frank Mason, director of the Office of Employee Relations, indicated that the state might be required to resort to "other measures" to bring an end to the strike. "Since the strike is clearly in a violation of the law and the union's contract, we believe we could resort to the injunction process."[48] On November 27 Mr. Mason came out more strongly for an injunction. He indicated that the students' actions at Kean College in seeking an injunction "were leading to a decision by the state to seek court assistance to end the walkout. He indicated he would meet today with college officials to determine whether an injunction should be sought."[49] In fact, it was later reported that "State officials completed preparations for going to court Wednesday afternoon (November 27, 1974). State college presidents and other administrators had provided the state Department of Higher Education with affidavits to be used in court in the effort to obtain injunctions."[50] Apparently, Monday, December 2, was the objective.

However, there was a lack of consensus on the administrative side concerning the use of the injunction. The state bargaining team, including the director of OER, officials from DHE, and three state college presidents supported the use of an injunction. The governor's office did not want to pursue this route. Governor Byrne, who had enjoyed solid support from organized labor in his successful election campaign, was extremely reluctant to antagonize labor by seeking an injunction against the union.

On November 27 the governor's counsel, Lewis Kaden, met with state AFT leadership until past midnight. The stories differ concerning who contacted whom for the meeting. The press indicated that the AFT sought out the governor's counsel.[51] But the AFT indicated that Kaden initiated the meeting. The significant point is that no other state officials were present. The eventual product of the meeting was the following seven-point agreement:

116

1. State and AFT agree to the appointment of Thomas Colosi of Washington, D.C., as mediator.

2. Negotiations under the direction of the mediator will begin promptly on all issues raised by either party within the authorization of the contract for the re-opener. At the option of the AFT, negotiations may begin with issue of librarians' rank and benefits.

3. The Council of N.J. State College Locals, AFT-AFL-CIO will recommend that the faculty return to full class schedules on Monday, December 2. The State agrees that there shall be no reprisals against employees, students, other persons.

4. The Governor and the AFT share a common goal—to preserve and expand the public higher education system in, New Jersey, to afford educational opportunities to all those who seek higher education, to maintain tuition costs, and thereby to preserve and expand job opportunities in higher education. The AFT supports the Governor's efforts to achieve these goals through legislative action to provide sufficient funds for higher education.

5. The State agrees to explore the following:
   (1) Revision of legislation to make available to individual employees who purchase them tax free annuities to the extent permitted by federal law;
   (2) Examination of pension options and benefits affecting higher education;
   (3) Contract administration procedures to encourage early resolution of grievances, including overload interpretations; with respect to federal grants and work during intersessions;
   (4) Rights of employees on leave to maintain health benefits at their own expense;
   (5) Procedures for regulation of leave for union service.

6. Make-up of lost time. Faculty members will be paid for Nov. 27, 28, 29.
   Procedures for make-up of lost time shall be implemented on each local campus. Such procedures shall include participation of the faculty members.
   On compensation for time actually made-up, the Governor states his support for the principle of pay for lost time made

up. He intends personally to investigate the question, to consider all the consequences, to hear the views of administrators and faculty, and to render a final decision on the extent and guidelines for compensation. The Governor will be guided by his support for the principle of payment for time made-up.

7. Negotiations will continue until an agreement is reached. If there is an agreement by the budget submission date, the budget as submitted will reflect the agreement. But negotiations may continue beyond February 1 if necessary, up to budget adoption and the terms of the agreement would then be submitted to the Legislature for inclusion in the budget.

None of the substantive contract issues causing the strike was resolved. The major dimensions of the agreement were procedural in nature: an outside mediator, a promise of back wages for time to be made up, and a promise to submit negotiated terms to the legislature for consideration. Although the agreement was not reached until late in the evening of November 27, and possibly early the next morning, the faculty were to be paid for that day, as well as the following two vacation days. Obviously, the promise of back wages and the three days' pay were intended to get the faculty to return to work. So, after having indicated at one point that only a full settlement of the contract issues would end the strike, the AFT signed a return-to-work agreement which resolved none of their contract demands.

SHORT-RUN IMPACT OF SETTLEMENT

The union appeared to be reasonably happy with the settlement in its public statements. The president indicated that the AFT had won the right to negotiate with this settlement. However, he was quoted as saying that the strike was only "suspended—not ended" and that the mass demonstration planned for the following Tuesday had been only temporarily postponed. He stated that the appointment of a mediator was a major bargaining gain.[52] He was quoted in another paper as indicating that the AFT reserved the right to call the strike again if settlement was not reached.[53]

The reaction of higher education administrators was immediate, and severely critical of the governor's actions in several respects.

In an article in the *Chronicle of Higher Education*, Chancellor Dungan termed "hogwash" the administration's position that seeking

118

an injunction against the striking faculty members would have hardened the union's position in the recent walkout. "What really happened was that Governor Byrne sought to be sure he will never in any future campaign activity be accused by a trade union leader of having brought in an injunction against a trade union," Dungan said.[54]

Of major concern to higher education administrators was their perception that educational policy decisions had been made by the political arm of state government, represented by the requirement that an opportunity be provided to the striking faculty to make up lost time and be paid for it. Chancellor Dungan stated that "if there is no price to pay, economic or otherwise, for the violation of the law and violation of the contract, then it's Nelly, bar the door! —there is no authority in the college presidents, in the state government or in the law itself." Chancellor Dungan said the settlement "confirmed a belief held by the union leadership that when push comes to shove, they can go directly to the governor and get things fixed up."[55] Statements by AFT officials that it had been necessary for Kaden to "engineer" the settlement due to the DHE's failure to bargain in good faith further angered state officials.[56] They felt that embarrassing the AFT was legitimate since the entire strike was illegal.

One source indicated that it was a matter of the state giving up $800,000 in back wages ($100,000 per day) to keep from having to issue an injunction, and that apparently the governor and his counsel thought it was a "reasonable trade-off." Since it was the first state unit to commence negotiations this year, the source noted that it would have been to the state's advantage to have beaten the AFT. The combination of the bad academic job market and an already favorable salary schedule would have kept faculty salary increases low, thus setting a reasonable pattern to use against other state employees. As noted in the previous chapter, however, there is some basis in history that a conservative bargaining posture by DHE and OER in the context of a relatively weak bargaining law was to some extent responsible for the greater degree of political involvement in the educational process.

Finally, the chancellor was angered because he had been supporting the governor in respect to budget priorities within the state. He was also furious because the governor's first public statement in sup-

119

port of higher education (item 4) had derived from the strike settlement.

The chancellor and the state college presidents demanded and received a meeting to discuss the settlement with the governor. In a meeting lasting one-and-three-quarter hours, the extremely angry presidents threatened to undermine that portion of the agreement calling for back wages. They thought it was a slap in the face for those faculty who had not gone out on strike to provide those who did strike with the full opportunity to make up lost time. They refused to certify the payroll for make-up wages.

Due to this resistance a December 2 letter to the chancellor from the governor's counsel, Lewis Kaden, said:

> It is and has been my understanding that the decision whether and to what extent any scheduled academic activity or any make-up of lost time as contemplated by item six of my statement is actually required is an educational judgment to be made by the President of each State College or his designee. No such activity will be recognized without approval of the President or his designee.
>
> In the event that time is actually made up, the completion of that work will be reported through the President and the Chancellor's Office to the Governor for ultimate determination as to the amount of compensation.

The dispute was eventually resolved in mediation by a compromise in which the faculty were paid for three of the seven days if the time was made up.

It was reported, however, that Kaden felt "the governor showed 'great responsibility' by intervening in the crisis. 'Our aim was to end the strike, not to provoke a confrontation. Now, maybe some people wanted a confrontation in court, and they believe they could have won it and crushed the strike effort, but we brought an end to the strike with no concessions and that was our goal.' "[57]

Whatever the validity of the relative positions, it seems clear that the AFT had been spared the uncertain impact of an injunction. Faculty support had started to erode and, given past precedent in New Jersey, the court would have issued an injunction despite the AFT's claims that the state had been bargaining in bad faith. Under an injunction the AFT's leverage to achieve wages for make-up time would have been reduced and negotiations would likely have continued as they have since the strike, but without payment for back wages.

120

The president of the state college locals was quoted as saying the "agreement offered 'an alternative to continuing a war. We're not kamikaze pilots.' "[58] But if the ANJSCF is successful in its recently announced campaign to unseat the AFT, then the AFT's misreading of the budget crisis will have been injurious to continued AFT leadership.

Meanwhile, negotiations with the outside mediator have continued without resolution (July, 1975). Despite the AFT's claims that the strike was only "furloughed," the contractual deadline of February 1 passed without fanfare because the legislature had not resolved the budget crisis with a new tax package. In fact, the legislature's Office of Fiscal Affairs has suggested a number of solutions to the budget problem. For example, it suggested that Jersey City State College should be closed down, and there were also rumors that another state college was being considered for closure. Also proposed were enrollment lids on all public institutions. The report had been ordered by a senator who wanted to know what the economic impact would be of closing one of the five state colleges in the northeastern part of the state.[59]

Under these conditions the odds were very small that a faculty bargaining agent representing a small percentage of state employees would be successful in bringing about the desired responses from the governor and the legislature.

NOTES

1 Agreement between The State of New Jersey and the Council of New Jersey State College Locals, February 22, 1974—June 30, 1976, Article III, p. 2.

2 Beth Fitzgerald, *Star Ledger*, November 10, 1974.

3 *Ibid.*

4 Richard Rosen, *Star Ledger*, November 18, 1974, p. 1.

5 *New York Times*, November 18, 1974, p. 37.

6 Barry Steiner, as quoted in Richard Rosen, *Star Ledger*, November 18, 1974, p. 1.

7 Frank Mason, as quoted in Robert J. Braun, *Star Ledger*, November 21, 1974, p. 51.

8 Information on history was obtained from individual college catalogs.

9 The Governor's Committee, *New Jersey Higher Education*, May, 1963, p. 22.

10 Department of Higher Education, "Enrollment Trends in New Jersey Colleges and Universities: 1965-1974," (Trenton, N.J.: Dept. of Higher Education, 1975).

11 For example, see Richard Carl Leone, *The Politics of Gubernatorial Leadership: Tax and Education Reform in New Jersey* (unpublished Ph.D. dissertation, Princeton University, 1969), pp. 173-325.

12 Barbara W. Doering, "Faculty Participation in Governance in the Transitional Teachers' Colleges" (unpublished M.S. thesis, Cornell University, 1969), p. 122.

13 The two new state colleges (Ramapo and Stockton) started up with faculty governance mechanisms.

14 P.E.R.C. No. 1, In the Matter of the State Colleges of New Jersey, April 9, 1969.

15 *NJEA Reporter*, May 28, 1969, p. 1.

16 Much of the following discussion is taken from: James P. Begin, "State-Institutional Relations Under Collective Bargaining in New Jersey," American Educational Research Association Symposium, Washington, D.C., April 1, 1975. (Mimeographed.)

17 N.J.S.A. 34:13A-8.1.

18 The Governor's Employee Relations Policy Council, consisting of the State Treasurer, Secretary of State, the President of the Civil Service Commission, Comptroller and Director of the Division of the Budget and Accounting, the Counsel to the Governor and the Director of the Office of Employee Relations, was established by Executive Order No. 3, April, 1970. The Office of Employee Relations was established by Executive Order No. 4 on the same date.

19 Suit filed in New Jersey Superior Court by the Association of New Jersey State College Faculty against the Employee Relations Policy Council, and the New Jersey Board of Higher Education and other public agencies, July, 1970.

20 112 N.J. Super. 237 (Law Div. 1970).

21 *Tenure at the State Colleges of New Jersey,* Department of Higher Education, June, 1972, p. 3.

22 64 N.J. 338 (1974).

23 A *Trenton Times* article indicated that while the NJEA and AFT opposed the tenure bill, "their lobbyists were not in much evidence yesterday. 'The bill would never have passed if the teacher unions had mounted a real campaign against it,' a senate official pointed out." *Trenton Times,* April 27, 1973, p. 9.

24 Robert J. Braun, *Star Ledger,* April 21, 1974, p. 1.

25 Interview with Marco Lacatena, June 23, 1975.

26 66 N.J. 72 (1974).

27 ANJSCF membership records.

28 The AFT subsequently changed its position and requested a statewide unit.

29 P.E.R.C. No. 72, In the Matter of State of New Jersey, et al., November 30, 1972.

30 Interview with Marco Lacatena, November 14, 1974.

31 Robert Bates, as quoted in Robert J. Braun, *Star Ledger,* November 21, 1974, p. 51.

32 Robert J. Braun, *Star Ledger,* April 20, 1975, p. 1.

33 The strike threat in February 1974 had been backed by a 3-1 faculty vote. The AFT explained the difference by indicating that last time it was only a threat, but this time there was a much greater probability of a strike.

34 Robert J. Braun, "The New Jersey Teachers Strike," *Change,* March, 1975, p. 25.

35 The questionnaire was a part of the larger study and was administered in the Fall of 1973 to a sample of faculty from all public institutions of higher education in the state.

36 Robert J. Braun, *Star Ledger,* November 19, 1974, p. 11.

37 Robert Nielsen and George F. Brickhouse, as quoted in Robert J. Braun, *Star Ledger,* November 24, 1974, p. 1.

38 Howard Parrish, as quoted in Robert J. Braun, *Star Ledger,* April 20, 1975, p. 1.

39 Walter H. Waggoner, *New York Times,* November 21, 1974, p. 51.

40 Joseph Britt, as quoted in Robert J. Braun, *Star Ledger,* November 27, 1974, p. 4.

41 Robert J. Braun, *Ibid.* Also Fred Heyer, *Trentonian,* November 22, 1974, p. 4.

42 *Rutgers Targum,* November 26, 1974.

43 *Star Ledger,* November 21, 1974, p. 21.

44 Henry Bryan, *Evening Times,* November 26, 1974, p. 2.

45 Robert J. Braun, *Star Ledger,* November 19, 1974, p. 11.

46 Marco Lacatena, as quoted in Richard Rosen, *Star Ledger,* November 18, 1974, p. 1.

47 Marco Lacatena, as quoted in Henry Bryan, *Evening Times,* November 26, 1974, p. 2.

48 Frank Mason, as quoted in Robert J. Braun, *Star Ledger,* November 24, 1974, p. 1.

49 Frank Mason, as quoted in Robert J. Braun, *Star Ledger,* November 27, 1974, p. 4.

50 Robert J. Braun, *Star Ledger,* December 1, 1974, p. 34.

51 *Ibid.*

52 *Star Ledger*, November 30, 1974, p. 1.

53 Ronald Sullivan, *New York Times*, November 29, 1974, p. 1.

54 Ralph A. Dungan, as quoted in Philip W. Semas, *Chronicle of Higher Education*, December 9, 1974, p. 2.

55 *Ibid.*

56 Robert J. Braun, *Star Ledger*, December 1, 1974, p. 34.

57 *Ibid.*

58 *Star Ledger*, November 30, 1974, p. 1.

59 Mike Piserchia, *Star Ledger*, March 26, 1975, p. 6.

Chapter IV

CONCLUDING OBSERVATIONS

THE CAUSES

The case studies of the two faculty strikes reported here tend to confirm the expectation that early faculty strikes will occur primarily where the issues are perceived by the faculty as directly and importantly related to the control of resources necessary for the acquisition or maintenance of professional status. While the nature of the conflict in the two strikes was somewhat different, and the outcomes very different, both strikes derived from a history of faculty frustration over the perceived absence of effective participation in decisions affecting their professional lives. (See Figure 7 for a comparison of the strikes, page 126.)

Pressures leading to the formation of the collective bargaining relationship and the subsequent strike at Rider College grew out of events and issues taking place over several years prior to the actual certification of the Rider chapter of the AAUP as the faculty bargaining agent. Severe disagreement developed between the faculty and administration over tenure and promotion policy, faculty evaluation procedures, appointment of administrators, and resource allocation.

Basic to the problems at Rider College was the attempt of the administration to bring about rapid improvements in institutional quality in a time frame and by means not agreeable to the faculty. After the president replaced a not-so-democratic predecessor who had led the institution for over thirty years, improvements were made in salary, the size of the faculty was increased in a time of declining enrollment, and the collegial mechanisms for decision making were improved with great emphasis placed upon their use. However, the collegial mechanisms also presented an opportunity for the faculty to define and set its priorities on goals, and to define the means and time constraints for achieving these goals. The president, confronted by these differences in priorities and means, felt constrained to push ahead and make decisions which were then perceived by the faculty as unilateral and arbitrary. These decisions then became the center of faculty senate discussions and set off a new round of disagreement between the faculty and the president—the president impatient with the faculty for not dealing with matters of academic importance and unhappy with the lack of rigor of their deliberations, the faculty replying that they could deal with such matters if the decisions arrived at through collegial mechanisms were respected and allowed to stand except in extenuating circumstances.

The faculty mistrust generated by heightened expectations for participation in decision making which subsequently were largely unmet, led them to adopt the one alternative perceived left to them for participation in decision making at Rider College—the establishment of a collective bargaining relationship. However, even the establishment of a collective bargaining unit and the subsequent negotiations did not result in the resolution of some important issues. With failure to reach agreement and the administration's unwillingness to grant further concessions, a strike ensued.

While these events took place in the context of the growth of a national faculty bargaining movement, the salient factors producing and shaping the Rider College bargaining relationship derived primarily from issues specific to the Rider faculty-administration relationship. For the most part, the impact of the faculty bargaining movement, which is especially strong in New Jersey, was to make bargaining a less unprofessional alternative since it had been accepted by many other faculty. Before the onset of the faculty bargaining movement the discrepancies in faculty-administration perspectives at Rider College and the resulting tensions might have been resolved differently, i.e., the president, confronted with a serious lack of confidence by the faculty, might have been eventually forced to resign. But in the collective bargaining era, other alternatives for action by the faculty have apparently been substituted.

The state college strike also derived from underlying faculty frustrations, but the different organizational structure gave the conflict a different pattern, and the state's economic situation produced a different outcome. Collective bargaining over a five-year period

Figure 7

Comparison of Two Strikes

	RIDER COLLEGE	NEW JERSEY STATE COLLEGES
	AAUP	AFT
Bargaining Agent		
Legality of Strike	Legal, under federal law	Illegal by state court decisions, but no legal action taken against AFT in this strike
Length of Strike	Six working days	Eight working days
History of Negotiations	Strike occurred after 13 months of negotiations for first contract	Strike occurred after four sessions in negotiations for third contract (AFT's second)
Causes of Strike	Deep organizational stress which led first to bargaining and then to strike. Specific issues were faculty evaluation, agency shop, status of department chairpersons and wage inequities. Economic condition of school not a major problem.	Wage and fringe benefit reopener. But perceived by AFT as an unfair labor practice strike. History of perceived conservative management bargaining posture reinforced by weak bargaining law built up frustrations which caused misreading of severity of budget crisis by AFT. Faculty concerned about job security and disposed to view state level of authority negatively. Strike not against local administrations. Economic condition of state a major problem.
Union Competition	None	An important worry to AFT given less than widespread acceptance of last agreement by faculty.

Level of Faculty Support	Overwhelming—bargaining teams had some difficulty controlling militancy in terms of getting agreement to settlement.	Good, but variable. Some erosion toward end.
National Support	Almost nonexistent. A reluctant visit by national official—small contribution to strike fund.	Major input to coordination of strike, national officials' presence very visible.
Role of Students	Made view known, some support of faculty wage demands but biggest influence was the potential rowdyism and negative effect on enrollments of a prolonged strike. Felt most by administration.	Unorganized statewide, with some in support of strike, some against. Did exert some pressure to settle by move to get injunction. Acquired self-interest as strike wore on. Little potential for loss of enrollment since entire system closed down.
Outcome	Resolution of issues of major importance to faculty. Classes madeup, no docking of pay.	No resolution of any contract issues. Got some makeup pay and outside mediator. Political interference in negotiations. Challenge of AFT by ANJSCF.

under two bargaining agents had produced little for the faculty, in part because the conservative bargaining stance of the state had not permitted the negotiations process to be used effectively to resolve a reasonable range of problems. There is some reason to believe as well that the relatively weak (from the union's perspective) New Jersey law limited the scope of negotiations and did not provide mechanisms for the proper ventilation of union frustration. It is worth noting that the Rider College faculty was able to achieve substantially more in its first contract than the state college faculty did over a five-year period.

To the extent that the weaker bargaining law had not enabled the reasonable resolution of faculty complaints, the state college strike was more a product of elements of the bargaining process than the Rider College strike. Whether a law similar to the federal law would have averted the build up of tension over the years and prevented the strike is a difficult question to answer, given the peculiar multidimensional structure of public sector decision making. In any event, these historical factors contributed to the AFT's misreading of the budget crisis. The faculty, concerned about the budget situation, particularly by the chancellor's statements in respect to budget priorities, and disposed by past history to believe AFT representations about state negotiations, supported the strike, but not to the same degree as the Rider faculty.

The causes of the strikes reported here are intimately related to the causes for organization in the first place. However, even among those faculty which have seen fit to organize for collective bargaining, the strike has not been adopted as an integral part of the negotiating process. The faculty still perceive the strike as the extreme and last effort to sensitize the administration to the faculty's position concerning participation in the decision-making process and the content of those decisions. At this point in time, faculty frustration not only has to have specific referents, i.e., concrete issues and/or persons, but the level of frustration has to be greatly heightened for strike activity to occur.

Whether or not strike activity will become an integral and normal aspect of the faculty collective bargaining process cannot be ascertained from these two case studies. However, continuing changes in the environmental context of higher education (e.g., declining enrollments and funding) will necessitate organizational adaptations to these environmental forces which may cause the factors important in the Rider College and the New Jersey State College strikes to surface in many other institutions as well.

In such situations the faculty may perceive that traditional mechanisms for their participation in institutional decision making are inadequate, and unionism and its ultimate weapon, the strike, while representing a militant alternative, may be perceived as the only alternative for gaining and/or maintaining control of those resources (e.g., salary, self-governance, tenure, etc.) important to the continuation of their professional well-being in increasingly bureaucratized institutions of higher education.

EFFECTIVENESS AND ORGANIZATIONAL IMPACT OF THE STRIKES

While the causes of the two strikes were related, the outcomes varied. The Rider faculty achieved the resolution of issues of major importance to them. The immediate effect of the authority redistribution resulting from the strike was to clear the air. Not only was unity brought to the faculty ("We did it!"), but, at least initially, improvements in the faculty-administration relationship were perceived by the parties. However, recent reports from the institution indicate that the battle lines are in the process of being re-established.

The gains of the state college faculty were procedural (make-up pay, mediation, provision for submitting eventual agreement to legislature for implementation); no contract issues were resolved. As a consequence, there is some possibility that the strike may contribute to another turnover in the bargaining agent. At least ANJSCF (NEA) thought it not inappropriate to announce soon after the strike its intention to turn out the AFT.

A comparison of the two strikes offers initial insights into the potential effect of contextual factors on the ability of faculty to inflict strikes costs.

The differing outcomes of the two strikes might produce a conclusion that strikes in the private institutions will be effective, and those in public institutions ineffective. While the outcome of the Rider College strike indicates that faculty bargaining power can be useful in resolving disputes in private institutions by affecting the distribution of faculty-administration authority, it is too early to draw conclusions concerning the differences between public and private institutions. Indeed, the major determinant of the differing outcomes appears to be related to economic and statutory considera-

129

tions, not structural factors. In a different economic context, recourse to the political elements of state government by the AFT might have been an effective tool. But the insensitivity of the AFT brought about by historical factors to the state budget crisis led to a less than satisfactory outcome in terms of the resolution of the contract issues. However, the strike led to political interference in the educational decision-making process, an outcome not generally possible in private institutions and one which was distressing to public higher education administrators.

Legislative differences between the two situations (strong private legislation versus weaker public legislation) not only had a varying effect on the causes of the strikes, as noted previously, but the apparent illegality of the state college strike made it more difficult for the AFT to carry through with its strategy because of the potential that an injunction would end the strike.

Differential effects of the bargaining structure were also evident. The multi-level nature of government organizations permits unions to bypass lower levels of management more easily. In the case of the state colleges, the conservative negotiation stance of the educational hierarchy led the AFT to involve political elements in negotiations in a major way, a redistribution of authority within the management hierarchy. While unions, in seeking the source of power, will often engage in end-running activities, the political elements of state government would likely be less responsive to union alternate bargaining activities when they are in agreement with the bargaining practices of the educational leadership. The state college strike indicated that political leadership will not be insensitive to a faculty strike in a public institution particularly when the governor is elected with substantial labor support and/or disagrees with the negotiating style of the lower levels of state management. At Rider College, the more compact management structure apparently made it easier to develop internal management consensus. AAUP contacts with the governing board indicated that the board and the administration were essentially in agreement on the substantive issues.

The varying bargaining structures and organizational structures in the two situations come together in an interesting way in respect to the role of the students. The fear of losing students was not a major concern to the administration in the state college strike. On the other hand, both the Rider College administration and the faculty were sensitive to the potential loss of students. The differing perceptions could derive from two factors. First, not all of the state college revenues come from tuition—not even a majority. Even though state college support from the state is enrollment driven, the effect of an enrollment drop is less extensive than at Rider College where tuition is the major source of revenue.

Second, the state college strike had closed all similar public institutions, making it somewhat more difficult for the students to transfer because of the higher cost of tuition in private institutions and out-of-state tuition in public institutions. But in a prolonged strike the students at Rider College would have had greater possibilities for transferring to other institutions at a similar or lower tuition cost.

The strikes indicated that the students do have significant potential for bringing about faculty-administration accommodations, both due to the possible effect of the strike on enrollments and to student activities during the strike to pressure the parties to settle. It was evident that students' self-interest about the potential loss of course credit became important as the strikes wore on. However, the large size of the state colleges made it more difficult for the students to organize themselves. As the students learn to orchestrate their activities to a greater degree, their impact is likely to be greater.

The two strikes would appear to dispel commonly held notions about the differences between the AFT and AAUP. As at Oakland University, the identification of the Rider faculty with the more "professional" AAUP did not deter the faculty from engaging in a strike. Apparently, if local conditions dictate the faculty will strike despite national affiliations, although in this instance the national AAUP leadership might find that the causes of the Rider strike would constitute "extenuating circumstances" under its policy. The experience at Rider and Oakland does indicate that local AAUP chapters can expect little strike assistance in comparison to AFT locals. On the other hand, the substantial presence of the national AFT in the state college strike was insufficient in itself to overcome the factors which conditioned the outcome of that strike.

What consequences will faculty strikes have for the traditional mechanisms for exercising faculty professionalism? Before collective bargaining the faculty in neither of these strike situations fully enjoyed the federated and collegial systems of faculty governance which have been described as representing the historical accommodation in many institutions between faculty as professionals and the bureaucratic organizations in which they work. So it cannot be concluded that the strikes in these institutions had undermined long-standing collegial mechanisms. Nevertheless, the question of faculty authority was paramount in both instances. The faculty saw the rationalization of policy resulting from the strike, for example, improved procedures for selecting department chairpersons as a means of ensuring procedures for effective faculty participation.

While the decision to strike created some cognitive dissonance among the faculty (striking is unprofessional), resolution of this dissonance was gained in the perception that not to strike would have been more unprofessional, i.e., a denial of their right as professionals to participate effectively in the decision-making processes that have an impact on them as professionals. In the state colleges, the fact that the strike was primarily a protest against external levels of management, and not local administrations, no doubt made the strike a more acceptable, more altruistic activity to the faculty.

Both case studies indicate that faculty will strike when confronted with issues of major importance to their working lives. This finding is important in itself since the willingness of faculty to strike is a necessary element of faculty bargaining power. Additionally the Rider experience suggests that the contextual factors in private institutions can occur in the right combination to enhance faculty bargaining power. However, the implications of the experiences in the state colleges for faculty bargaining power in public institutions are less clear. A more accurate reading by the AFT of the economic situation in New Jersey might have prevented a strike or produced a different outcome. But the absence of the right to strike in New Jersey and the threat of an injunction make such statements speculative. Further understanding of the forces affecting the ability of faculty to strike successfully in a public system awaits the analysis of other faculty strike experiences.

STRIKES AND STRIKE MANAGEMENT
IN HIGHER EDUCATION

A Selected Bibliography

General

American Federation of Teachers
A practical but almost complete guide for the striking college
teacher. Washington, D.C., 1969.

American Society for Personnel Administrators
Strike preparation manual. Berea, Ohio, 1974.

Carr, R. K., and D. K. Van Eyck
"The strike and the academic profession." In: *Collective bargaining
comes to the campus,* American Council on Education, 1973.

"Faculty participation in strikes." *AAUP Bulletin,* Summer 1968,
pp. 155-159.

Hutchinson, J. G.
Management under strike conditions. Holt, 1966.

Hutt, W. H.
The strike-threat system; the economic consequences of collective
bargaining. Arlington House, 1973.

Kadish, S. H.
"The strike and the professoriate." In: *Dimensions of Acadamic
Freedom,* University of Illinois Press, 1969.

Lozier, L.
"Changing attitudes toward the use of strikes in higher education."
Journal of the College and University Personnel Association, April
1974, pp. 41-48.

Paterson, L. T., and J. Liebert
Management strike handbook. International Personnel Management
Association, 1974. (PERL No. 47)

Roberts, K.
"Operating after a strike begins." In: Marceau, L. (ed.) *Dealing
with a union,* American Management Association, 1969.

Roberts, K.
"Planning for operations during a strike." In: Marceau, L. (ed.)
Dealing with a union, American Management Association, 1969.

Saso, C. D.
Coping with public employee strikes. Public Personnel Association,
1970.

Cases

"Allegheny County [Pa.] Community College reopens after agreement on new contract." *Government Employment Relations Report,* Report 473, 1972, p. B-20.

Bunzel, J. H.
"Faculty strike at San Francisco State College." *AAUP Bulletin,* September 1971, pp. 341-351.

"Chicago [Junior Colleges] strike ends in pay raise." *Chronicle of Higher Education,* January 13, 1967, p. 3.

"Faculty ends strike at Chicago City [College]." *Chronicle of Higher Education,* October 1, 1973, p. 1.

Feinsinger, P., and J. Roe
"The University of Wisconsin Madison campus—TAA dispute of 1969-70, a case study." *Wisconsin Law Review,* 1971 (1), pp. 229-274.

"Lake Michigan dismisses 54 faculty members over faculty strike." *Chronicle of Higher Education,* March 19, 1973, p. 2.

"New Jersey college teachers end strike [State Colleges]." *Educator's Negotiating Service,* January 1, 1975, pp. 79-80.

"Professors on the picket line [Westmoreland County Community College]." *Chronicle of Higher Education,* May 21, 1973, p. 5.

Semas, P. W.
"Law officers open Antioch [College], ending six-week strike." *Chronicle of Higher Education,* June 18, 1973, p. 3.

Semas, P. W.
"3 colleges settle strike [Wayne County Community College, Westmoreland Community College and Chicago City College]." *Chronicle of Higher Education,* September 24, 1973, p. 3.

"Story of one strike; organization of the teaching assistants at the University of Wisconsin." *College Management,* July 1970, pp. 15-17.

"Story of one strike that shut down Eastern Michigan University." *College Management,* December 1970, p. 7.

"Tacoma [Community] College teachers conclude nine-day strike." *Chronicle of Higher Education,* November 5, 1973, p. 2.

"University of Delaware ends one-day walkout." *Government Employment Relations Report,* Report 517, 1973, p. B-18.

Van der Water, Peter, and L. Sattrelle
"Ten lessons learned from a strike [St. Lawrence University]." *College Management,* February 1974, pp. 12-14.

Additional copies of ACADEMICS ON STRIKE may be ordered from:

> Library
> IMLR
> Ryders Lane
> New Brunswick, N. J. 08903

Other publications concerning related topics may also be purchased from the library.

Academics at the Bargaining Table: Early Experience. Proceedings of a conference. 31 pages. James P. Begin, editor.

Faculty Bargaining: A Conceptual Discussion. 68 pages. A research report by James P. Begin.

ORDER FORM

Please send copies of the following books.

☐ Academics on Strike $5.00
☐ Academics at the Bargaining Table: Early Experience .. $2.00
☐ Faculty Bargaining: A Conceptual Discussion $2.50

I enclose a check for .... made payable to Rutgers University. (New Jersey residents add 5 percent sales tax.)

Name ....

Address ....

City .... State ....

ZIP

 2